On Anxiety: An Anthology

3 of Cups Press

Published in 2018 by
3 of Cups Press
London

References to websites were correct at the time of writing.

Paperback ISBN 9781999877606

Printed and bound by CPI Group (UK) Ltd, Croydon, CR0 4YY
Cover design by Harriet Smelt & Clare Bogen

www.3ofcups.co.uk

Introduction

I wanted to publish an anthology about anxiety because it kept cropping up in conversation. I was diagnosed with anxiety disorder as a teenager; however, it wasn't until relatively recently that I started to hear about it from others.

Anxiety has become somewhat of a modern buzzword. Yet, a quick google tells you that even the ancient Greek philosophers grappled with it. And while we've evolved from accusing sufferers of witchcraft, or calling it 'irritable heart syndrome', it is just as, if not more, relevant today to investigate. When we first sent out a tweet calling for submissions, we were blown away by the response and support. Anxiety is universal, regardless of background, race, gender identity or sexuality. I was most touched by how many of you reached out to us with enthusiasm; it felt like there was a lot of room, and need, for more art and writing on mental health and, specifically, anxiety.

In the current political and economic climate, it is no wonder that we're all feeling a bit anxious. Unfortunately, with recent cuts to the NHS (and looming changes to the US healthcare system) a lot of us aren't able to get the support or care we need. Often the first step to tackling mental health is to talk about it; I hope this anthology gives insight into the various and diverse faces of anxiety. This book is not a resource (although we have provided a resource page if you want to investigate further, see page 147) but it is meant to start a broader conversation about mental health.

This anthology is very close to my heart, and I want to give special thanks to our contributors who were willing to tackle a difficult, and very personal, subject.

Clare Bogen,
Founding Editor
3 of Cups Press

Contents

The Mania of Wakefulness

Sarvat Hasin

Not sleeping is a hell of a thing.
Hemingway

1.
It becomes a haunting. Your body remembers sleeping the same way soldiers in wartime movies remember their childhood sweethearts: with the fear they will never see her again or smell the perfume in the crook of her neck as they kiss. You are afraid. Sleep is just out of reach and you wonder if it will always be that way. Can you forget how to do something so instinctive? Can you unlearn that trick where your brain switches off from your body, floating away in the dark while the rest of you is still there – breathing, tossing and grunting alone?

2.
The first time I told a boss that I'd forgotten how to sleep, he looked back at me with a glaze of disbelief.

'Sometimes,' he said, 'When I can't sleep I look at the clock and see what time it is. I feel as if I've been lying awake for about forty minutes but when I look at the clock again, it's almost two hours later. So I must have been sleeping, right? Do you think that's what's happening to you? Maybe you just don't realise when you've been sleeping.'

I want to say I was surprised by this but I was not.

3.
There is something unbearably private about not sleeping. Checking your watch becomes a maths problem. You calculate how long you have: one o'clock – if I fell asleep right now I could sleep five hours before I have to be awake. Two o'clock – four. Three – three, four – two.

Five – one.

4.

People always ask me if I write in the hours I cannot sleep. In fact, they do not ask. Rather they congratulate me on the finding of time, as if I have discovered the hours between one and five in the morning just for myself, to build worlds in. It seems useless to explain, for they must know, that there is no way that three hours of work, no matter how holy, can replace a night's sleep. They must see, by now, the circles of grey and blue smudged under my eyes like a bruise. From how I throw back cup after cup of coffee or the days when my hands begin to twitch.

Writing, when it is going well, is better than coffee. If I wrote in the night, it would be as if I were giving up on even the sly hope of sleep.

5.

It was around the time that sleeping was at its most elusive that I took up boxing. A friend, who shared some of my affliction and who suffered from night terrors, and ran to keep them at bay, said: 'We're all just toddlers. You have to tire yourself out before bed.'

But I was already tired. I didn't think it would work. I didn't think it could but I was, at this point, desperate. Over the years, I'd tried everything. I'd given up coffee. I'd slept on pillows sprayed with lavender. I'd tried meditation music. I'd tried honey. Valerian. Magnesium. Some trick with breathing and clicking your tongue that I found on Google at half-past three that just made my mouth dry and made me so mad. My parents sent me articles and I wanted to send them back, with all the different things they'd suggested crossed out because I'd done those before – I'd tried them all.

In the meantime, I was getting more wound up, living on a frantic, fast-dwindling supply of adrenaline. My hours were cluttered with restlessness and then I got out of bed at six in the morning to write before work, crafting weird, mad stories in those dark January hours, on my lunch break, after work. I didn't really get out much. I got sick all the time, my immune system worn out from not sleeping. I fell prey to every strain of cold and flu circling through London. I felt, not for the first time, as if my body was betraying me. I spent the hours of wakefulness in the dark room a hostage to my body's determination to stay awake, to never get comfortable, no matter how many times I flipped the pillow or changed position, to my brain's inability to stop running through a litany of things that worried me.

I'd been around enough people who waxed lyrical about the benefits of physical exercise, the rush of these mythical endorphins that filled their body after a workout. I'd never been athletic. Nothing I'd ever dabbled in had worked. I did ballet for a year and enjoyed the discipline of it, of how it made my body feel strong, balanced and less clumsy. But that was not the same thing they were talking about, the flooding of good feeling in your muscles. It wasn't until I started boxing that I really got it: what it could be to spend an hour with your brain washed clean. Nothing to focus on but the way you moved. Burying yourself in the technicalities of each punch: where your feet should go or how to move fast without falling over. I walked home drenched in sweat under my winter coat, feeling the sort of giddiness that women seem to have after first kisses in romantic comedies. Like a slow, warm blush spreading out over my skin, a light going on inside me. I sang in the shower. I hit the bed and fell deeply into sleep's dark, warm arms.

6.

By the time you've lived seventy-five years, you have possibly slept for twenty-five, twenty if you work hard. That is a third of our lives spent under the veil of dark, sweet nothingness, rolled into balls and cocooned out of consciousness. It seems so natural when it is happening to you, but from outside the kingdom of sleep, it becomes quickly bizarre.

Before a trip to Berlin, a few years ago, I tried to cure myself of not sleeping by cutting coffee out of my life. It didn't help: now I was just cranky and sleepless, sniffing friends' cappuccinos like a weirdo. But I think I enjoyed the martyrdom, so I could point to this pain – the headaches I got in the afternoon from breaking up with coffee, how everything was fuzzy for longer in the mornings – as proof of my devotion to sleep. Look, I wanted to say, *I'm trying*.

And then, six of us crowded into a small flat, I listened to the breathing of other people: the snoring, the yawns, the girl who giggled in her sleep. How weird that their bodies were still here while they were somewhere else. I quit quitting when, after a particularly rowdy night at a heavy-metal bar, we planned to go to Museum Island.

I couldn't face the paintings without a cup of coffee.

7.

I wish I could write in the hours I don't sleep. I'm anxious already about the speed at which life goes past and about not making the most of it. I could learn languages in the time I don't sleep or read *War and Peace* all over again. If I weren't a woman, I'd probably take up walking and learn London in the dark, teaching myself all the routes between tube stops that I don't have time for in the day. I could start my own fight club. I could take up knitting, make bread, finally cultivate the kind of hobbies that make people seem interesting at dinner parties.

Instead, when I get bored of tossing and turning, I watch terrible television and pass out in the early morning with my face smushed into the keys of my laptop. A much less romantic use of this gift of time.

8.

Sleeplessness seems passive when you talk about it, but in the grip it is plainly aggressive, hacking away at your composure for weeks at a time.

My bedroom is haunted by the night before, by the unbearable heat of my bed and the memory of tossing and turning. Suddenly, there are monsters under my bed. I do not want to go into my bedroom, or into my bed and I most definitely do not want to turn off the lights. Insomnia has crawled out of my chest, from the little thumping thing behind my ribs to a hulking beast that stalks around the dark of my room. He plays with the nerves in my legs to keep them jumping in the night. In his low, barely there voice, he sings all the things that went wrong with my day and all the things that could go wrong tomorrow. He reminds me of that thing I said at a party when I was twelve, that thing that was so embarrassing but my daytime self would never ever remember. I grow flushed and throw off the sheets. I feel him sitting on my throat, squeezing the moisture from it until I am parched and have to get up again. I drink water by the window and though I do not turn around, I can feel him dragging his body over my bed, spreading bad dreams on my sheets so that if I catch a few hours as the sun comes up, they are full of violent jerks, my blood leaping, eyes shot through with colour.

9.

I have developed a wariness over the years for cures. Things that worked once may not work again. Meditation music was hypnotic when I first discovered it. It knocked me out as cleanly as prescription sleeping pills for a whole week before I built an immunity to it. I have kept sleep journals, writing notes to myself about the quality of each evening but that got boring fast. Charting patterns intentionally is actually more unusual than you would imagine. I realise that I have been measuring wakefulness for years. There are times in my life that have been coloured by how the nature of my sleep accompanied them: holidays remembered fondly even if it rained every day and we got lost, just because I slept fully every night. Times of happiness that seemed bad because I couldn't sleep the night before a big day: a friend's wedding, the day of my first book launch.

These days I listen to podcasts in the night. It is my latest trick. I don't rely on it, I know better than that, but it's comforting to lie awake with other people's voices in your head, telling you stories. It keeps the beast at bay and makes the hours until morning less grim. I know people who listen to *Harry Potter* audiobooks in bed, or the radio. I think perhaps it is something about the act of listening that is so comforting. It's almost as if I can forget why I'm there, bundled in a dark room to do anything other than listen to people talk about books or movies. I pick the funny ones for bedtime and make my body still as a trap, trying to catch sleep out in the moments of listening. It doesn't feel as violent as before, not something that hangs over me constantly – a spectre that must be chased away, banished by some incantation or potion.

Sleeplessness and I live side by side. There are times when I can predict its rhythms – I never expect to sleep well before a job interview or when sharing a bed with another person, a new variable in the already delicate dynamic – and times when it gears up unexpectedly.

For better or worse, I can do without sleep now – though not for long stretches of time. A bad night here or there doesn't crush me the way it used to. I battle the fatigue in the day rather than obsessing myself with the beast of the night. I know to shower as soon as I wake up, to hydrate, to get out in the sun for as long as possible to fool my brain into thinking it is time to be AWAKE, to pace myself between cups of coffee and not go for a sugar rush straight after lunch. I can make it through the day, write, read, go to work, hold a conversation, box, cook, the lazy business of everyday – and think somewhere around the middle of the afternoon: *There. That wasn't so bad, was it?*

Chuchotage

Ka Bradley

Paula Fevre had not replied to her email. The email had been sent eight days ago, a hasty, multi-font, copy-and-paste collage that drew liberally from draft emails written several months ago that she had never sent. It was vital that Paula Fevre responded to her email of eight days ago, or else the guilt she felt in not sending the email sooner would itch.

Waiting for the email to arrive – as it surely would, at 23:46 on a Monday night – she was flicking between Reddit and WhatsApp Web.

Into a message box she typed:

'I'm reading this thread about a 25F whose boyfriend [24M] has an entire porn folder filled with girls with ass+ length hair'

A spider of unusual rotundity and gravity had constructed a web between the two aloe vera plants succumbing to despair at the window. As she typed – she hit the keys hard – the flat-pack desk shuddered under the impact, sending minute vibrations along the windowsill. The spider twitched expectantly every fourth or fifth keystroke. It reminded her of her mother when she first got a mobile phone; she would jump with the urgency of someone shouted to every time the phone buzzed. 'Oh, a message!' her mother would say, in the French pronunciation. 'Oh, a message!' every time for months.

Two blue ticks. She typed:

'the issue is not so much that he watches porn (she's taken pains to assure us she also likes porn) but that she doesn't understand the ploriferation of this one attribute or what it means re: the particular bent of his desires'

'*proliferation'

'I thought it quite a harmless and charming kink tbqh'

Two grey ticks. She typed:

'I had more thoughts about this re: the image repertoire and the literal use of repertoire trimmed of intimacy in contemporary pornography but also I am tired and must sleep NOW and will see you tomorrow GOOD NIGHT xx'

She stayed up for a further eighty minutes, combing through the strands of other people's misery. Paula Fevre was unforthcoming.

***

The next day, at lunch, Celine said, 'Please don't write an essay about RedTube and Barthes.'

She chased a piece of tofu around the plate, hampered by sauce. 'Huh?'

'You were sending me stuff about a Reddit thread last night...?'

'Oh. That. Sorry. I was just... Noodling.'

Celine wore glasses that were slightly too large, both in frame and fit. They made her look like a belligerent owl. She could feel Celine regarding her stonily over the top of them, and tried to remind herself that it was not severity but the bad luck of ill fit that made Celine peer so.

'And between the noodling,' Celine said, 'have you had time to look over the copy editor's notes?'

'I don't want to lie to you.'

'So?'

'But I will if I have to.'

Celine sighed and leaned back. 'You know that, as well as being your editor, I am also your friend.'

'Yes, Celí. You remind me every time I make you angry.'

Celine pushed her glasses up her nose. 'There are production deadlines to meet, proofreaders I would prefer not to piss off.'

'Yes, Celí. I'm sorry.'

'Don't look so ashamed, it's unbearable. You loved writing this one, remember! You have to return to that love. I still listen to the voicemail you sent me when you first had the idea for it. The flow of it, the precision! A violent dissection of modern love, with that wonderful mythological framework.'

'Yes, Celí.'

'Stop saying "yes, Celí" as if you were my henpecked husband. I am shouting at you because I believe in you. In fact, I am barely shouting.'

'Yes, Ce– I mean. Not. I'm sorry. Don't tell me off for apologising too.' She put down her chopsticks. She often wondered about the presence of chopsticks in certain South East Asian restaurants, whether it was another example of the endemic Orientalising attitude to Asian foods in the Western world. In Thailand, Cambodia and Laos, spoons and forks, or hands (dish-dependent), are used for eating rice. Chopsticks are for noodles, and the Chinese and Vietnamese. She'd put down her chopsticks thinking about this and now she looked up at Celine.

'The thing about making a modern version of an old story, though, is that, everything has already been said.'

Celine studied her. 'Everything that can be said has already been said,' she replied. 'OK? You'll kill yourself trying to be the first at something. There is no original language left. There is only the experience of the melody. Isn't there? Say, "Yes, Celí."'

***

She visited her mother.

'But tvear,' her mother hollered as she turned stepped through the front door, to which she still had a key.

'I'm coming through the door, maey. I'm in the process of shutting.'

'Did you read my tex?' Her mother didn't pronounce the 't' of text.

'I haven't looked at my phone.'

'I'm trying to download *Only Fool and Horses* from the unternet.' Singular fool, a mangled Francophone pronunciation of 'internet'. 'It was your father favourite. I watch it to feel close to him.'

Her father had been dead for two years. 'Yes... I... Why don't you just buy the DVDs? They'll be better quality. I can buy it for you. You don't know where this has come from.' She peered over at the screen, with her coat and backpack still on; she'd begun to sweat in the skin-prickling heat of the house, harassed by duty and warmth. 'Mum, this is just some pirate streaming site!'

Her mother, who had sucked her lips in with concentration until she looked like a thoughtful coconut, released them with a splutter of scorn. 'Who buys DVDs?' she scoffed, making a sarcastic effort with the sibilants. 'It is a rip off. Your brother make a Netflix programme for me, to never buy DVD again. Buy the DVD! You are making a mick.'

There was a withering twinkle, a dying light dying down, in her mother's eyes. Her mother knew the idiom wasn't 'making a mick', probably. Probably her mother also knew that when she said maey that she always put it in italics in her head, preferred 'Mum' unless she was making a point. Her mother wasn't the only one working with a risible accent in a foreign language.

When her father was dying, he began to lose his mind linearly, dropping one year after another until he'd run out of English-speaking ones. His twenty-something-year-old mind had panicked, curdling in a bedridden sixty-something body. His mind was wifeless and childless. 'Chmou ei?' he'd asked her with terrified newness, every time she'd entered the bedroom. 'Anak chmou ei?'

'Channeary,' she'd replied, first through tears and eventually, as the disease wore on, tiredness. 'Knyom chmou Channeary.'

He'd respond in sentences beyond guesswork. Fear and vocabulary barricaded him in. This was the price her father paid for the nativisation of his children. He died in confusion, as lost as if he'd been tossed into the sky. Before speech abandoned him altogether he'd started calling her mother lok yeay. Her mother had cried hardest then.

'I'm not even a real grandmother yet!' her mother had wept, and the shame tugged at her so hard she tore her eyebrows out while she slept. But what can you say to comfort a parent? They bring you into the world to weep over you, it's inevitable.

***

She checked her emails over dinner. The first time she'd done this, visiting home during her father's illness, her mother had responded with characteristic explosive rage.

'I cook you this fuckun dinner and you sit there and press the button! No love! No sharing! No appreciation!'

'I need to check my emails,' she had replied, half-choked with a sudden, matching, abrupt fury. 'Do you think I want to be like this?

I'm so busy, so fucking busy. Everyone needs something from me.'

'Don't fuckun swear to me,' her mother had screamed, entirely unironically. 'I cook dinner and you just press the button and eat like a zombie. You would have no care if it was shit. You eat like you live in the shit.'

Her mother pronounced 'the' as 'der'. In der shit. In truth, home had felt like a shit heap, with her dying father upstairs, the housework neglected in favour of the more pressing task of ministering to his decline. After his death, her mother had cleaned everything, throwing out half the house. Everyday, she thought of an object that reminded her slightly of her father, missing it, knowing it had fallen to the fire of her mother's grieving mania. Der shit, disposed of. She knew, and wished she didn't, that her mother had thrown out her own mother's letters after reading them. Not out of callousness, but out of tidiness. Even sent across the oceans to this cold and sopping land, they were merely correspondence. Letters were DIY fixes; they patched the problems over until real conversation could put the head in working order. With her mother dead, her husband dead, stopgaps were grotesquely useless.

Now, over the food, her mother simply looked up and asked mildly, 'Why are you press the buttons?'

'I'm waiting for an email.'

'Who?'

'Paula Fevre. The translator?'

'Who translate Ty Phok Phalla?'

'Yeah, that's right.'

Her mother used a thumb to push rice into a temporary structure of salted fish and cucumber dammed against her fingers, before lifting the whole thing to her mouth. 'I am so pleased you are writing a story about Ty Phok Phalla. My favourite writer.'

She smiled. 'I know. But you know I'm not writing about him. I'm using one of his poems as the inspiration for the new book. The one about the king who keeps pissing off his wife in a new form every time he's reincarnated.'

'Yes, I'm sorry, my English, that's what I mean. Who is Phalla Fev? Very coincidence with the name, the same sound.'

'I used her translation of the poem as source material, because I can't read the original, and I quote from it at the beginning of every chapter. I need to clear permission to use it, and, to be honest, I just wanted to acknowledge how important her translation was to me.'

Her mother shrugged. 'She will be please to be in a new book, maybe make some money for her.'

'Maybe.' Celine, with a sort of gleeful despair, had shown her how punishing permissions fees could be, so she was hoping not. But she was glad to have overcome her months-long shyness to finally be able to write and say: 'look, you speak what should be my first language better than me, and you've saved me, you've given me a bridge home.' She had imagined several times what it would feel like to be Paula Fevre, knowing her translation of an obscure epic poem in an obscure language had inspired an entire novel, hoping there would be a sense of pride, even maternal protectiveness. She had visualised winning some award for the book, thanking Paula Fevre profusely for being the springboard she had bounced from.

'Your father would be very proud.' Fardder; prout.

'I hope so.' Her father had wanted her to do a law degree.

***

That night she had bad dreams. In them, she and Paula Fevre argued in French, in French that was (for her) fluent but consisting of four or five phonemes, as (it turned out in the dream) French did. She was explaining why she hadn't gotten in touch with Paula Fevre sooner, but struggled to find the vocabulary in the primitive, underdeveloped language of French to do it. This awful, awful tongue, she dreamthought. Why do they teach it in British secondary schools? You can hardly ask for the time in it. Is it because it's so simple that it's the only language the British will learn?

Later in the dream, she was being woken up on the day of her father's funeral. Her mother was asking if she had the reading prepared. But she had not prepared any reading. She scrabbled around her childhood room, looking for something suitable to honour her father – her flesh and blood, her rock, the man who had taught her how to pick the ripest wild sloes, who had carefully dyed the hair of her Sindy doll black for her when she was a little girl – aghast and ashamed at having left it to the last minute, but all she could find were endless collections of Byron's erotic poetry. I can't go to the funeral, she dream-thought wildly. I can't go to the funeral with this!

When she woke, it took several minutes for the horror of that shame to leave her. Something of it lingered in a way that felt prescient. She rolled over, slapped a hand around her bedside table until it hit her phone and tapped in the code to wake it. Paula Fevre had replied.

Dear Channeary,

I am currently in the U.S. and have only just had a chance to read your email. I am writing to tell you now that I cannot and will not endorse this project, and to express my shock that you have not made any attempt to reach out before now, to me, to my agent, or to my publisher.

What you have described is tantamount to intellectual property theft. Your novel would not exist without my translation. What you describe as 'inspiration' is plagiarism. I do not give you permission to quote any part of my translation in 'your' book. I am astonished that you could not find a more original subject. Do I put this down to inexperience, or dishonesty?

I have copied in my agent and my editor. We expect to hear from you imminently.

Regards,

P. Fevre

She was wailing, 'Muuuuuum!' before she realised she'd even found her voice.

She heard her mother hammer up the stairs. 'What? What happen?' She fumbled with the door handle. 'Kdoi pak. Channeary, what happen? Are you hurt?'

Her mother pronounced 'what' as 'vot' and that syllable was so much more desperate and scared. She started to cry. 'Mum, I'm in so much trouble. Maey, I'm in so much trouble.'

Her mother was still in pyjamas (Care Bears, a faded-beyond-legibility label declaring it suitable for 12–13 year olds in the neck; her mother was small). A plummy smell of sleep hung around her. 'Why?' Vhy? 'It cannot be so bad. Tax? Deadline at work? You have your health!' The open panic in her mother's voice made her feel sick. To resort to platitudes within a matter of sentences surely suggested a crime beyond reasonable conversation.

'Paula Fevre won't let me quote her, and she says I stole from her! I can't publish this book! What will I do? It's already come back from the copy editor! What will I tell everyone?'

Her mother sat heavily on the bed. 'How do you steal from her?' she asked, wonderingly. 'She does not own Ty Phok Phalla.'

'I worked from her translation–'

'But you write the book yourself?'

'It's not that simple,' she sniffed, starting to get annoyed despite herself. 'It's intellectual property.'

'I don't know what that mean,' her mother said helplessly. 'She will sue you?'

'I don't know, Mum.'

They sat side by side, one out of the duvet, one in. The phone was clutched loosely in her hand; it started to buzz as the emails came in.

'I will help,' her mother said. Then: 'I am very proud of you. Like your father. You are a good writer. I don't know what this woman want. You always have many idea, many way of explaining things, especially to me, when I am old and stupid. This woman is wrong, as simple as that.'

'It's not that simple,' she repeated, but her throat had gummed up with tears. She put her head against her mother's shoulder and waited for a wail to come, but all that came was silence. They sat like that for several minutes, listening to the neighbour outside whistle back at the blackbirds as if he thought they could understand him.

Claire Gamble Normal Service Will Resume Shortly

3 Poems

P.E. Garcia

an anxious american at marble arch

listen buddy the blood   that has been fl owing has start ed
to coagu   late

every last man   on earth is   starving

& i'm just sitting here like,

                    what the fuck y'all up to tonight

a guy on the tube keeps asking to go home
but his friends say *no no*
                                        no

words are drop ping   like over   ripe fruits

we were under   ground & albert was in gold
just sitting there like,

                    who says death is only a darkness

meanwhile all the tour   ists are trying to find
the way
out

& i'm standing under marble   arch asking
        all the history   to make some meaning

for the rot   ten   fruit i keep
crumb   ling   in my   hands

P.E. Garcia

Charles I with His Head Stitched Back on

Look: skull all pomegranate
  bloody,

  mouth red from confessing
  seeds

  of time gone
  poison

  & the eye of the bloom.

are you my king?

Hear: suckle-sweet voice
  preaching

  an apple blossom
  apocalypse

  & crown thorns
  covered

  in rosepetal&cork

you are not my king

Forgive: axe its blade
    needle its prick
    blood its stain

Forgive: people mindless
   wandering cruelty
   of casual bureaucracy

See: their eyes have been
  dreaming spires & hands
  knitting star-covered skulls
 with tongues poisoned
  & crying
  & crying

what was i
without you

you are my king,
you are mine

        the one i belong to

P.E. Garcia

Omphale

call me fair

            Clarinda

or Salomé,   kissing
          the lips of Iokanaan,

or Omphale, holding

the snake, drenched

in rosewater&honey,

   holding

an olivewood

club & draped in lion's skin

paint   my   nails   in   godsblood

for you
      see:

          one of my great loves
          was unseen:

          i, on my knees,
          before the trembling

man

Alignment

Sophie Mackintosh

I was in my late teens when, for a short period, I started wearing oven gloves while I slept. I was very afraid that I was going to hurt somebody I loved in my sleep. I had no desire to do this in my waking life which, at the time, was miserable. This misery spilled over and made the fear – a compulsive, icy fear – even worse. My body felt completely unknowable. So did my brain. I was thinking for the first time, *what am I capable of?* I was coming face-to-face with what my body would and wouldn't do.

In the daytime, when I wasn't stacking shelves, I lay in the grass of my childhood home and stared at the sky, hands twisting into soil. Long summer holiday. When I was at work, the fluorescent lights spiralled something in me. I saw meaning and pattern in the labels of beans, of soups, and wanted to cry at the tenderness of it all. At the *what-is-the-point-ness* of it all. At night, I put heavy objects against my door, the gloves on my hands.

Every night I was surely too afraid to sleep, but I would eventually drop off. In the morning, I was lying in the same place, though I had worked the gloves off. Everybody I loved was always still completely fine.

***

There is a long list of ways to self-soothe the terrible electricity of your brain, and I'm sure if you're reading this you're familiar with them. You do not need a list of destructive coping mechanisms. But I no longer want to obliterate. I actually want to do what's best for my body these days, now I am older, sadder and wiser. Now I scroll, click, scroll again. I listen to white noise when the world feels overwhelming, or the same song again and again and again. I breathe deeply. I make lists for everything, purely for the dopamine ping experienced when I tick something off – a small and easy reward. I check several horoscopes a day.

***

I became obsessed with my horoscope at thirteen, when I got my first, devastating crush. I couldn't walk down the corridors at school. Instead, I hid in the toilets all lunch time, such was my abject terror of seeing him. On the bus ride to school, where he sat at the back, I listened to music too loudly through headphones and pretended he did not exist.

The only refuge other than music, apart from lunchtimes spent with a book in a toilet cubicle, was my horoscope. I read them in my mother's magazines and then in the teenage magazines I asked her to buy for me, an attempt to be less of a weirdo. I read the beauty tips alongside the horoscopes. *Your crush is waiting!* I experimented with brown and blue eyeshadow and persuaded my mother to pay for rimless glasses and highlights – six harsh, orange streaks in my hair. *Things will get better!* But even my attempts at being normal were hopeless. What teenager asks for rimless glasses because they seem less conspicuous? I looked like a newsreader. This is a good week for love! It was never a good week for love. Yet I kept reading.

***

Sometimes my hunger for horoscopes grows insatiable. The usual sources are not enough. They are too vague, or too specific even, and I then need to find another one. Sometimes I cheat – I look at next week's horoscope in advance, for example. On holiday in Australia at the end of 2016, more depressed than I had been in a long time, my heart pounding inside the shell of my chest, my mother took pity on me and spent eight dollars on a 2017 guide for me. We were in a hot, flat resort in the middle of the desert. My head jellied and soft with jetlag, I read the whole year in one sitting. I felt like I was skipping ahead on my future, looking at what I shouldn't look at. The horoscopes said, *This year will be a good one for you.* There at the tail end of 2016 I thought, Please, and I washed my hands with sulphur-smelling water and a tiny eucalyptus soap in the bathroom, and watched a television show about killer animals tearing each other apart.

The best part was when the horoscope said *From October 2017 and all through until November 2018 you are entering a golden phase*, and this did lessen my anxiety for a moment, this kind of specificity. A snake reared up and killed another snake. There is nothing to worry about, I told myself. All of this, all of the empty hours, the nights lying awake, the early mornings, the searing pain in my chest, the panic attacks, it will add up to something. There is something bigger than you. There is some sort of plan. I didn't dare to explore the question of *so if there isn't, then what the fuck is the point?* I didn't feel the need to open that box.

***

Anxiety is the failure of the body to submit to what will be. To what could be. There are a hundred possibilities of what could happen to me and to the people I love and my brain conjures up the worst of them. Some of the worst of them have happened. So in that sense, reassurance can seem futile. Our bodies are proof of this day after day. The news is proof.

And it's shitty to live like that, with your pain balled up inside you like a wet tissue; with no map for what to do with it and no coping mechanisms other than the ones that hurt you or the people around you. Checking my horoscope is benign at worst. At best, it forces me to think about what characteristics I possess and how I step inside the world. *Does my ascendant make me inflexible? Yes, maybe it does. Could I be less intense or kinder? I don't want this attribute to belong to me. But does it?*

***

Astrology engenders a sense of communion, whereas anxiety is isolating. I swap star charts with my oldest friend, born the day before me. We are a good example of how you can be the same and yet dramatically different. Individual planets and alignments and times work upon a person. We read our horoscope together and we both identify. There are two freckles on each of our forearms that we used to believe were proof that we had been somehow joined together cosmically, back in the days when we used to sit on the ragged folding seats in our high-school auditorium at lunchtimes (way past hiding in the cubicles), my nails bitten and painted black, her hair down to her waistband. When I tell her these days about how Venus retrograde is completely fucking me up, for example, she understands, she agrees, she is feeling it too, those imperceptible vibrations in the air, that pre-ordained logic.

I am sitting at her hospital bed with a copy of *Spirit and Destiny*, the only vaguely astrological thing I could find in our small Welsh town. Her and my mother share different but strangely similar chronic diseases, and she has been admitted while they fight the inflammation raging through her body. It wasn't the plan; she is on holiday, living usually in Sydney, but our bodies don't care about plans. Anxiety thrums along the ward. It's eclipse season. We disregard the parts of the magazine that focus on angel sightings, on crystals and orbs and skip to the horoscopes, where we read that eclipse season means *healing, new beginnings*. 'Well, I should hope so,' my friend says to me, picking the skin off a wizened potato.

***

My mother is also into astrology. She is a Libra. I am a Scorpio with Virgo ascendant, moon in Aries and Libra in Venus. It's her heritage to me. I am scared that she is going to die. In-between visits to the hospital to see my friend, I lie on the sofa with my mother and watch television programmes like *Ghost Hunters* and *Come Dine with Me* under a blanket. We take long walks on the beach. She French-braids my hair. I am so scared that she is going to die. Libras are graceful, beautiful, good at social situations, garrulous. My mother is all of these things. We are in the car when she starts to cry hysterically from the pain radiating throughout her jawline, the first time I have ever seen her cry from physical pain. I am so fucking scared that she is going to die. A cracked tooth, a routine operation, a cold, a million things, all could undo her. Everyday objects glow to me with a secret malignancy when we're together. What if that vase were to fall on her foot? What if there is mould on the sliced bread we've been eating all day? When we're not together I read her horoscope down the phone and listen to her turning the predictions over and over.

***

The horoscope never says, *You are going to die*. It never says, *The people you love are going to die*, though we know that both are true, eventually. The horoscope is the purest instrument of hope that I know.

***

Anxiety is a feature of my mental illness, sure, but it's also a totally natural response to everything that happens in the world. Sometimes I think that instead of being a cowerer, a cringer, I should be rampaging on the streets. I should be doing whatever I want, kissing and dancing and shrieking, because aren't we all going to die anyway? The horoscopes are big on integrity and doing *the difficult things*. If we're all fucked anyway, and even if we're not, wouldn't I like to go out with a bang, the horoscope implies? Would it have been so difficult to live with no fear? To have told the people you loved that you loved them all the time, to keep that certainty inside them, beautiful and insoluble as a pearl? In the perfect world of the horoscope, one always does the right thing. Anxiety is embraced as a precursor to change, to taking the leap into being a better person.

***

It's inevitable that we put some sort of faith in signs and symbols, dense and mysterious as theorems. What else is there in this slippery world? We all want to be told how the story will end. We are all blindly feeling our way through the dark. It is very soothing sometimes to feel that I am putting my trust in something bigger than myself. It's a second off from the responsibility for my life and all that is contained within it.

And is it such a coincidence, really, that the two happiest romantic affairs of my life have been with people that share a birthday, both Capricorns, historically a great Scorpio match? And is it such a coincidence that my dear best friend, oldest and wisest, is born, as noted above, on the day before me? Is it a coincidence that the best thing that has ever happened to me started to take place when the full moon was in my sign? But then, maybe this is just part of my compulsion to assign meaning to literally everything, the constant quest to unpeel the skin of the universe where it sticks. And if I want to believe that life, my life, can contain a sort of magic, what is the harm in that? It gets me through my days.

***

The day my mother cries in front of me with pain the first time is the same the day that the Pleiades meteor shower peaks, which also happens to be the birthday of my younger sister (a total Leo). By the evening, the pain has passed temporarily. My mother is back in herself. My oldest friend has been discharged from the hospital earlier that day, after two weeks inside. Things seem to be settling.

At eleven, we turn off the television and move into the garden. I text my friend about the meteor shower. Twenty or so miles away, she stands in her own garden with her hospital wristband still on. We are never normally looking at the same patch of sky; it is luck, good and bad, that has brought us both home at this particular time and changed our plans. Luck that I have left my job in the last few days and can now go anywhere, in theory. Bad luck that we are not in London together at this moment, the original plan for the evening. Luck that it is this particular night where the meteors will fall through the sky.

Horoscopes, when they coincide, are just that, maybe; coincidence, luck. Though you could forgive me for daring to believe, sometimes, that the universe might have some sort of plan for us. The stars are always telling me to work harder, to dig, but also to submit. The ball of anxiety in my chest opens up like a fist, then closes back in. Things are going to happen to me. And I am going to let them.

***

My mother and father and I crane our necks until it is painful.

They live under one of Europe's clearest night skies. I can see the constellations sharply: the fog of the milky way; Orion and his belt; Cassiopeia; the Plough.

Then the shooting stars start. They are large, and they flame. They are pieces of untouched yet proven science. But their magic is inescapable, a thing to bow down before. There is calm for the first time in this day of phone calls, of car journeys, of doctor appointments and exhaustion. We wait for the sky to be done, and we are silent.

Crossing Borders

Nicole Froio

One day, my mother sat us down to talk. I don't remember how old I was, but I know that we were going to travel to the United States soon to visit my mother's family. My brother and I listened carefully to my mother, a Latina woman who had crossed borders plenty of times in her life.

'Don't say anything to the border officer,' she commanded. 'Only answer to them if they ask you something directly and don't answer more than required. We don't owe them anything, we have visitor visas and nothing to hide.'

We both nodded and my mother gave an especially significant look to my younger brother, who tended to talk too much. At the time I didn't understand why she was coaching us, and we crossed the border from Brazil into the United States without any issue as far as I was aware. This wasn't the only time she cautioned us about how to act while going through border control, it happened in some form or other every time we travelled. She led by example, resisting blatant attempts of provocation by border control agents, and always reminded us of the initial talk we had that day.

Years later, as an adult, I remembered this coaching as I waited to go through border control into the UK. My chest was tight at the prospect of being duly questioned by an officer who would decide whether to let me in or not. As I waited, I noticed a Brazilian boy crying alone, only accompanied by an immigration officer who looked mildly annoyed at having to deal with him. The boy tried to explain, between terrified sobs, that his father was British and that he was visiting him for the first time.

I felt sorry for him, remembering that my own mother had taught me throughout my life to stay calm, only answer what is asked of me, and ignore any rudeness or deliberate attempts to provoke. I wondered if his British father had any idea about what crossing UK border control felt like for non-EU nationals, if he noticed it has become progressively more stressful, as I have in the last six years I've been travelling. Does a white British man notice the growing narrative of unwelcomeness immigrants have been subject to for years? Does he understand this might be a traumatic experience for his child? Or is he simply waiting in arrivals, assuming everything will run smoothly because his passport privilege insulates him from questioning?

As those questions swirled around in my mind, I focused on my breathing because my turn was coming up. I prayed for a nice border control agent, gripping my folder of so many corroborating documents giving reasons for my stay in the UK. My anxiety feels like nausea, a tight chest and a foggy mind all at the same time, and I breathe in and out to settle my thoughts and my body.

Even writing about these experiences triggers physical reactions. Writing this essay has been a stunted process: I started and stopped about a hundred times, unsure of whether my feelings are valid or important. The physical borders that I must cross have built borders in my mind: both the physical and imagined borders limit my space, behaviour and worth. My intrusive thoughts reshape who I am, how I act to fit the borders that define acceptable behaviour, which stands in opposition to 'foreign' behaviour, that which does not fit the hegemony. It is not only that those borders disassociate my body from my mind because of the fear I am harbouring when crossing them; it is that the unwelcomeness those borders signify have made a home in my head and I carry them everywhere I go.

***

When the Tories scrapped the post-study work visa seemingly the minute they were elected, they effectively closed the door in my face and I had to come to terms with the fact that I would be forced to leave the life I made for myself while I was studying as an undergrad in Sheffield.

My first panic attack happened shortly after I realised I could no longer stay. It was like something inside of me had broken. The future I had been envisioning suddenly disappeared before my eyes, despite all the work I had put into it. My chest started hurting, like a permanent heartache I would be unable to shake for the following three years. I felt trapped, like my options had evaporated. Looking back, I realise that something inside me had, indeed, broken: the illusory belief that I belonged in the UK, cultural differences and all, was gone and my mind struggled to replace it.

After moving out of the UK, I came back to visit my then-boyfriend in 2014. This was the first time I would be entering the UK since I graduated and moved back to Brazil. It felt familiar to be coming back, to be walking the floors of Heathrow Airport, following the signs that say BORDER CONTROL and joining the ALL OTHER PASSPORTS queue as opposed to the EU PASSPORTS one.

However familiar the space felt, the whole process was also deeply restrictive. The border control officer asked me what I was doing there, I answered I was visiting my boyfriend. This seemed to set off alarm bells in his head. A woman from the global south, a brown woman, visiting her British boyfriend?!

'How much money did you bring? Do you have a job in Brazil? What do you do? Do you have a letter from your employer?'

I had a steady job at the time, but I had never been asked to provide a letter from my employer to prove that I had a job. The answers I gave were unsatisfactory, the bricks of unwelcomeness were being stacked with every wrong answer I gave him. I had been through this so many times, and I was still treated as if I was doing something dishonest for simply travelling with a non-EU passport. Finally, the officer asked me something that makes me angry to this very day.

'What's your boyfriend's phone number so I can confirm what you are telling me is true?'

Somehow, I managed to feign serenity and write down my boyfriend's number. I didn't burst into the angry tears my anxious, heavy chest was demanding. I pretended that having a second person corroborating my story was a completely normal thing to be asked. I pretended that having a chaperone in my boyfriend wasn't completely demeaning, stripping me of my individuality and personhood.

He instructed me to wait in a makeshift waiting area: a few seats in front of the officers' booths. I sat down, feeling like something was stuck in my throat. I bounced my right leg up and down. I messaged my parents, letting them know I was waiting to be let in, bracing myself for the possibility of being forced onto a plane back to Brazil for eleven hours.

The officer came back, said my boyfriend had confirmed my story and reluctantly let me back into the UK. I started breathing again, and as soon as I was out of his sight, I cried. I had felt as scared as that little boy I saw crying. Generally, however, adults are supposed to pretend that everything is fine, that being surveilled and questioned is a normal part of our day that doesn't rattle us. That little boy's reaction was provoked, it wasn't just a childish overreaction.

In hindsight, this was the beginning of internalising borders as a limitation of behaviour and an aspect of my anxiety. These non-physical borders force me to overthink my actions and my expressions, lest I seem too foreign. The borders in my head make sure that my origins don't shine through in visibly transgressive ways that would disturb British hegemony. The borders in my head are more flexible than the physical ones I am forced to respect no matter what: they can bend and open if I trust someone enough, but they are always there.

***

That summer, my boyfriend and I travelled to Paris and Amsterdam from London. Even though we had already travelled together, even though I had just been through a harrowing experience at border control in the UK (an experience he had been a part of), even though last time we travelled together I told him it would be best if we went through the border together – he still went to the EU passport queue alone and I went through the non-EU passport queue separately. At one point, one of the border control officers on my way out of Paris asked: 'Where's your boyfriend?' and I had to explain that he had an EU passport and that he had gone through the other queue.

The thing about privilege is that you don't notice it's there until someone pokes at it enough. I had a conversation with my boyfriend and pointed out how easy it was for him to cross European borders with his passport, and how it was a little more complicated for me with a South American passport. It was possibly my annoyance that finally got through to him, but up until that moment he hadn't truly realised the privilege that comes with carrying a passport that isn't suspicious. There were no borders in his mind.

I know that I am privileged: I am a woman of color, I am brown. European and American people tend to racialise me both because of the tone of my skin and my nationality, but I am also light-skinned and white passing. I am from the global south, but I am also middle class and able to travel. I am an immigrant in the UK presently, but I am a student immigrant – I am not a refugee, I am not an economic migrant. I know that my experiences at the border(s) are not as bad as what a lot of other folks go through.

But I also know that my passport comes with context and warnings. I know that I thought I was welcome in a country and then, I realised that I was not and that my presence there was contingent upon politics beyond my control. I know that xenophobia and racism aren't going away anytime soon. In fact, it seems like these sentiments are getting stronger by the day and that a border-less world won't ever exist. I know that my own position as an international student is a model of 'the good immigrant', that my position is slightly more secure than asylum seekers – but still, the general air of unwelcomeness that is part of the fabric of British society inevitably hits me too.

Soon, I am travelling back to the UK to continue my PhD study. I am already dreading the interaction at the border. Most of all, I am tired of coming back to a place that blatantly doesn't want me. I am tired of having to brace myself for possible expressions of contempt at the border and inside the border.

I came back to the UK at the end of 2015 because I wanted to do an MA in Women's Studies and Brazil didn't have many courses that catered to what I was looking for. Visa applications are always long and incredibly invasive. People from the global south who apply for student visas for the UK have to give specifics about their finances and travel history in the past decade. When I was applying to come back, it felt like I was going back to an abusive boyfriend, trading independence and citizenship in my own country for surveillance and suspicion to get the degree I wanted. It was certainly a choice that I made, and as uncomfortable as it felt in 2015, Brexit hadn't happened yet and it was about to get much, much worse.

In 2016, when the majority of British voters chose Brexit, the borders in my head thrived and expanded. The weight of the xenophobia and racism embedded into that referendum was such that I became more uncertain, and worse, I heavily questioned my own worth and right to be in the UK. My rights and my worth, in fact were – and sometimes still are – entwined with each other, which is something I would never impose on anybody but myself. Outwardly, I became unsure of who I could trust to be pro-immigrant and anti-racist, and redoubled my efforts not to offend the hegemony. Inwardly, I questioned my own anti-racist positions. Surrounded by mainstream discourses about the white working class and immigrants stealing their jobs, I thought that there must be a reason why xenophobic and racist rhetoric had become so powerful, and deep inside I asked: could it be that I have no right to be here? Were people right in scapegoating me and others like me because we were draining housing and work from British people?

I wonder if the borders in my head will ever be dismantled. I have always believed that freedom of movement is a human right, but the solidity of crossing legal borders led me to internalise those borders, even if I didn't believe in them, they were there. In my head, they manifested as social limits to my interactions because of an extreme anxiety of being rejected not only by the border control officers, but by British culture and people. In person, British people always tell me that it is not a personal rejection of who I am, but being an immigrant in Britain has become an important part of my identity, and will continue to be so for as long as I live here, for as long as the rhetoric is xenophobic and the borders are material.

***

Sometimes, I am able to relax and forget about the borders, but then something happens to remind me that I am different and only here on borrowed time. After an evening hanging out with a friend at her house, I thought it would be safest to call a taxi to get home. The driver was a few minutes late but I didn't think anything of it. He explained, in a slurred voice, that he had gone to the wrong address. I laughed nervously as I told him my address and assured him that it was fine and I wasn't in a rush.

'Where are you from?' he asked, obviously curious about my accent.

'Brazil,' I answered, keeping my answer short and hoping he would understand this as a plea for silence. If he understood this, he ignored what I was asking for: he continued to ask me questions about my ethnicity and nationality that are now blurry in my memory. Soon enough, I found myself listening to a racist soliloquy of Latina stereotypes.

'You all sounds so angry when you speak Spanish,' he laughed. 'Sometimes I see groups of you and it's like you're all fighting! I never want to cross Latin women, not me.'

I shifted in my seat, uncomfortable, and forced myself to laugh. At this point, I was fairly sure he was either drunk or on drugs, and I desperately wanted to avoid escalating the situation. I clutched my keys in my hand, doing the keys-through-knuckles fist well-known to women in case I needed to defend myself. He kept on babbling about what he thought about Latina women and how loud and passionate we are, but everything he said blurred into my desperate need to get out of that car as soon as possible.

He finally pulled up to my block of flats. I quickly handed him the money I owed and left the car, but not before he told me to 'Dump [my] boyfriend', and I was forced to laugh nervously once again to placate his offensive and incomprehensible babble.

This is how the borders follow me everywhere I go. The markers of difference are in my accent, my skin colour, my hair, and people wonder what I am, where I am from. Explaining myself is tiring all on its own without having to humour blatantly racist taxi drivers for my own safety. That conversation is an extreme example of how immigrants are always asked to explain who we are, why we are here, and, most importantly, where we are really from –because we don't fit with the hegemony, these credentials are necessary, even owed, to the British people I encounter.

Such questions wouldn't be so intrusive and upsetting if the current conversation about immigration wasn't so hostile and hateful. The conversation becomes charged with invisible power dynamics that inevitably trigger my anxiety, and, much like when I'm going through border control, I become desperate to give the right answers, the answers that will allow me to stop explaining and just exist.

Redefining Anxiety

Dr. Rachel Kowert

Pre-show jitters. Transitory nervous laughter. A lifetime fear of clowns. All of these experiences refer to the same underlying state: anxiety.

While anxiety is a term that is often used colloquially, misinformation and misunderstanding surrounding anxiety and anxiety disorders varies widely. This includes confusion on how best to define anxiety (in fact, there are entire books dedicated to this topic) as well as how anxiety can be, and is, experienced.

Is anxiety best defined as an exaggerated threat response to a non-threatening situation? Or should it be framed as a psychological condition underpinned by an existential crisis? Or maybe a superstition created and perpetuated by society? Is it all of these things? Or none of these things?

Three common myths and misinterpretations about anxiety

Anxiety is not a genuine problem

Within society, anxiety is often minimalised as either a temporary condition (such as performance anxiety) or a childlike phobia (such as coulrophobia, a fear of clowns). In some cases, this might be true. For instance, performance anxiety often wanes once the performance has started, whilst a fear of clowns may cause high anxiety no matter one's age or situation. However, reducing anxiety to this dichotomy mistakably frames all experiences of anxiety as either temporary, fleeting episodes or as a lifetime of problems underpinned by childhood trauma.

While the previous examples of performance anxiety and phobias are anxiety driven, minimising anxiety to these two categories also disregards the range of chronic anxiety disorders that many suffer from, such as panic disorder, social anxiety disorder and generalised anxiety disorder.

Anxiety is something you can just 'snap out of'

Many assume that people who are experiencing extreme anxiety can simply 'snap out of it'. This misperception likely comes from the misunderstanding of how anxiety is physically manifested. The experience of anxiety is deeply rooted in our nervous system and spans our physical, psychological and behavioural response systems (more on this later).

For example, individuals with agoraphobia (fear of situations where there is no safe or easy way to get away, such as crowded public places or public transportation), often report that if they leave their house they may become overwhelmed, paralysed with fear and unable to move. In these situations, it is not possible to simply 'snap out' of this state of extreme anxiety. However, through cognitive behavioural therapy (CBT) and intervention training, individuals can learn various strategies to utilise in these kinds of situations.

Anxiety is experienced unilaterally

This is perhaps the most persistent and problematic assumption about anxiety. While anxiety is generally understood as feelings of worry, nervousness or unease, how anxiety is manifested and experienced differs depending on the person and the situation and is influenced by both genetic and environmental factors. For example, feelings of anxiety can be brought on by a specific event (such as speaking in front of a large crowd of people), an uncertain outcome (such as being unsure whether air travel is safe) or both.

Defining anxiety is difficult; however, psychologists have noted several underlying consistencies across most experiences of anxiety.

What is anxiety and how is it experienced?

Anxiety is intrinsically linked to our fight or flight response system. Generally speaking, anxiety is a normal response to a perceived danger or a threat. Feelings of anxiety are integrated through psychological (i.e. feelings of nervousness, anxiety and panic), physical (i.e. release of the neurochemicals adrenaline and noradrenaline, increased sweating, heart palpitations, etc.) and behavioural (i.e. pacing, avoidance, etc.) systems that work together when a threat is detected.

If anxiety becomes chronic, overwhelming and/or detrimental to daily activities it is often labelled an anxiety disorder. The behavioural symptoms associated with anxiety are more pronounced during these excessive states of apprehension, as these feelings typically coincide with compulsive behaviour and/or panic attacks. While there are dozens of specific anxiety disorders, some of the most well-known include social phobia, post-traumatic stress disorder (PTSD) and obsessive-compulsive disorder (OCD).

While there are similar characteristics underpinning all experiences of anxiety, the opinion that there is a singular right definition or experience of anxiety could not be further from the truth. Anxiety can be many different things and experienced in many different ways. For example, from a psychological perspective, anxiety may be framed as a combination of physiological and psychological processes that have manifested into a specific emotional state of high anxiety. Depending on the psychological perspective of the therapist, the underlying circumstances that drive this state of high anxiety could be attributed to difficulties in finding meaning in life's challenges (existential perspective), unresolved conflicts with the self or others (Freudian perspective) or a range of other previous experiences.

Physiologically, anxiety can also manifest itself in many ways. Anxiety can be situational or chronic; it can last a few moments or a lifetime.

When experiencing anxiety, individuals may start blushing, sweating excessively, have difficulty swallowing or sleeping, feel nauseous, begin shaking involuntarily (voice, hands, etc.), experience muscle tension, have facial tics, a racing heartbeat, extreme dizziness and/or a sudden rise in blood pressure, among others. Some forms of anxiety are associated with one specific physiological response (such as blushing when experiencing performance anxiety), whilst others can include a range of symptoms (such as sweating, difficulty sleeping, racing heartbeat and high blood pressure when suffering from PTSD). However, the symptoms encountered by each individual experience of anxiety can – and often does – vary.

What does this tell us about anxiety?

Acknowledging that anxiety is a multi-faceted concept that includes a range of physiological, psychological and behavioural components is the first step towards accepting that it is not a singular experience or concept that can be explained by unilateral generalisations. It is also important to remember that everyone encounters feelings of anxiety from time to time. It is an integral part of the human experience. For instance, we have all felt a surge in blood pressure when the teacher calls our name in class and we are unsure of the answer, or the tingly butterflies before a first date with someone we really like.

However, for many, anxiety can be a more chronic and debilitating experience, with states of high anxiety persisting across many situations and failing to dissipate over time. Unfortunately, there is no 'magic cure' for high anxiety. For some, coping techniques that are learned and refined through formal training may work best, whilst for others more informal meditation and breathing techniques may help make the symptoms of anxiety more manageable. It is important to remember that there is no 'one size fits all' treatment and finding the best solution for any particular person will likely take some trial and error.

Until the right solution is found, people suffering from high anxiety may find comfort in the fact that there is no one singular right or wrong way to experience anxiety and they are not alone. We can get through it together.

Coast in Breezes

Hannah Williams

[Content Note: Sex, Compulsive Behaviour]

The language of superstition is coated on my youth, as thick as the mist that lies on the hillsides and slips down in the dusk. The distinctive hill of my childhood, flat-topped and ending in an unexpectedly elegant curve of scree and moor, was the site of seventeenth-century witch trials. Each year, on Halloween, people still walk up to the summit, dressed in cheap cloaks and pointed polyester hats. I always wondered if they were surprised by the ferocity of the wind at the top or the angle of the rain that usually falls at that time of year. Snow remains on the hill long after it has melted in the valley.

I always walked up a different route, one that began with soft wet grass and turfed foothills, and led up to a well set in the hillside, surrounded by heather and rocks soft with moss and spotted with lichen. At a vantage point near the top of the hill I would turn and look out over the wide valley, at the fields strung together and the tops of mountains in the distance. The name of Pendle Hill is a repetition. In Saxon, in Cumbrian, in modern-English, a three-time hill rolling over the valleys of the tongue.

One
Two
Three

***

Look back and forth. It is difficult to satiate myself, to convince myself to disregard intuition, need, want. OCD thrives on significance, on the belief that an inconsequential act can have power. A negative thought becomes a promise, a curse, a plague on my house. But if I can repeat that moment, perform that action again, as many times as I need, then I can prevent what I have done. An undoing. A spell weaved through constant repetition, to soothe. It took time, but I knew I must always make time for something so important.

Bashall Brook, River Hodder, Dinkley Brook, River Dunsop, River Loud, Pendleton Brook, Sabden Brook, Skirden Beck, Stock

Beck, Stydd Brook; the tributaries of the River Ribble. It is the Ribble that gifts the area with its name and defines the land with syllables like water over pebbles. It is the Ribble that flows through the region, dividing and creating and shaping as it goes. There are spots where I dived in summer, where the banks are sprinkled with mayflowers and daisies and the buttery scent of gorse, and the water is churned by whirlpools and currents. A place of ascents and descents, hills and valleys. I am its daughter, plunging my hands in the cold water of the river again and again until they are numb.

It started with charms and rituals used as they have always been used; to keep away the dark. In winter, the clouds are heavy and full of rain and it is dark by 4pm. How could I fail to see this as a portent?

I am a child of witch country.

One knock on wood if I thought of something that worried me. That's a fair trade – a quick tap in exchange for safety. The pleasing security of the clunk that signals a fingertip against something solid. The sound that means I can exhale, releasing the breath I found ballooning in my chest. If I am going to tap once, I should tap thrice: three is a charmed number, and what are we dealing with if not charms?

There are rules. No MDF, or plastic with wood grain, or plywood. No touching my head as substitute. Paper is allowed if there is truly nothing else available. Different types of wood are a good omen and a resource that should be used.

There were always more things to do to ensure that I was safe, and once I had thought of them I couldn't stop. They became a part of my routine, talismans against my own thoughts. I don't come from a religious family, but I did attend a Church of England primary school. Every night I prayed, first for everybody to be safe and then, when that wasn't enough, I named members of my family, even the ones I wasn't close to and wasn't overly concerned about, which of course meant that I had to pray even harder. I'd mumble into the dark, my hands clasped together and my eyelids pressed shut, as though the force of my own body could signal my contrition. I'd pray in front of the window, facing the hill behind my house, the stretching fields, and feel my pleas reflected back to me in the valley.

***

When I was sixteen, my hips and thighs already streaked with shell-pink stretch marks, I met the boy I would date for the next three years. Our clumsy romance, all bitten fingernails and early morning texts, stumbled along. At the start we'd sit in the graveyard near sixth form and I'd sit on his lap whilst we kissed, startling in our innocence. Feeling for something whose shape I did not recognise, amongst the long grass and the headstones.

We were never in love, but I was haunted by its outline – a reflexive yearning, performed day-in, day-out. I think I got halfway there, with affection, with intimacy. When I felt doubt I repeated my actions until they coordinated with thoughts of love, as though this would erase the sins of my fears. But I could never stop doubting and I could never be full. I desired so much that it made me sick.

After we stopped having sex, we stopped going outside. He didn't want to fuck me, so every time I visited I ate potato cakes on his bed, closed the curtains against the sun and played video games with orange-rendered sunsets brighter than those disappearing behind the fells, my fingers greased with butter.

When I visited him in Brighton we watched the tide and ate chips looking at the skeleton of the West Pier, giddy from playing penny-games in the arcade. I could believe then that I loved him, my wish granted from washing my hands repeatedly in too hot water the day before. It lasted as long as I could hear the sea. We travelled back to his too small student room and the smell of heat against the cheap fabric made me nauseous. I started to bleed lightly, undramatically, after sex. During the night I woke up with a UTI and spent my return train journey doubled over, my carton of cranberry juice leaking onto my dress. I only realised when I saw the stain bleed through the fabric.

***

I moved to the city, and my loneliness ensured that I had time for penitence. I scrubbed my hands 'til raw, drank water 'til I choked. I sat in the dark in my room because I could not stop myself from flipping the light switch, like a hangnail you cannot help but peel. The city was dark and rain slicked, seven hills to close around me seven times. I lived in a drafty, early twentieth-century student block where leaves blew up the stairs and into our shower room and I watched Netflix until 4am, taking three hours to watch a twenty-minute episode that I rewound and replayed, over and over. I was constantly late for lectures. The hills outside my room became steeper everyday, until I was too exhausted to climb them. I went home, most weekends, by train, the windows falling open as it rattled through the moors.

When I was nineteen, I moved across the sea. I slept for most of the flight on my mother's lap, legs curled underneath me. On the descent into Stockholm I saw endless pines, forests pitted with lakes. From our height they could've been fallen acorns or peach stones, the size of my thumb curled over.

Stockholm is made up of fourteen islands, situated where Lake Mälaren meets the Baltic Sea. It does not have the strung-together nature of Venice, crumbling and spitting out water and brick as it sinks into the sea. Instead it luxuriates in its space; the archipelago has some 30,000 islands, framed by blue and green and blue again. The breeze comes in from the lake, softened, and carries the scent of fir and sea salt. I ate fried herrings with dill and mustard sauce at the weekends. My hands unknotted. I felt my body linger in a way I had not allowed it to before.

I fell in love with the city because it was always between.

I drank wine on friends' balconies, lay back on different mattresses, ate pittas stuffed with falafel and pickled peppers and danced whilst looking at the pink streak of dawn. I still checked the knobs on the front of the oven, still rotated them before I left the apartment, still walked around the park near my flat at 2am, lighting a joint with jittery hands because I felt too awake, too tense. But it was no longer primary, no longer resting in the tips of my fingers and the ends of my nails. At the end of one night I ran down the street to the apartment of a girl I was on a date with, both of us singing Velvet Underground songs, connected by shared headphones and clasped hands. I did not think of the light switch or the lock on my door or the oven dial.

When I came back to the UK, leaving behind the city that had become part of my sinews and muscles and that now I could only look at as a blurred image on Google Maps, my anxiety returned like an illness, an old wound rising to infection. I rented a small student house in Sheffield with a freezing attic room, sharing the sterile kitchen and mildewed lounge with two people I did not know. I was ill constantly, cold and crying and repeating almost every action for hours. I washed and scrubbed and picked and hurt, all of me raw. I no longer tried to conceal my tics, turning my head to look out of my skylight over the city in the dark until my neck ached.

When I met my partner and I moved to another, nicer, part of the city, with leaves on the streets and an antique bookcase in my room, and made friends who didn't leave me on read receipts, I expected my mind to mellow and soften. I had traded the wind-blasted hills of the north for the rounded names of Psalter Lane and Cherry Tree Road, but the city was the same. I walked downhill, feet getting faster.

It is difficult to believe that my interpretations are not entirely correct, that there may be no deeper inquiry. I questioned until the truth appeared to me, unequivocally. Questioned and weighed and deliberated all that I knew, as if by holding it up to the light I could see the stain. Sometimes my questioning was successful, and I would feel my flesh flood with bliss.

I analysed and deconstructed constantly, retracing thoughts until I became lost, my mind terrifying in both its foreignness and familiarity. My mind looped onto the roads and paths and rivers of the city, the routes I walked every day, and I wandered through them lost, stumbling. I pulled myself apart with heartbroken ferocity. There were nights where I screamed myself breathless on the stairs and lay bent over in the bathroom, folding in on myself from the pain. I believed that I was damned.

***

Uprooting. To pluck my limbs from the ground and fling them far, lest they settle back in the same soil. I never think of leaving as fleeing, though I have fled people and things. My periapt is now the silver pill packet in my bedside drawer, *Citalopram 20mg Tablets Sandoz Ltd* written all over like a charm. They have crossed sea and boundary, always with me.

I moved to London to feel vast; to drink in a bar of unknown faces and watch flocks of green parakeets fly over Brockwell Park. I found myself swimming, submerging my body in the dark green of the pond at Hampstead Heath, the freedom of cold water against warm flesh. I cupped the flowers, fat and bright, that grow along our new road. Half Moon, Winterbrook, Beecroft, Brightling, I cycle down roads that have become the connecting lines of my palm.

The pollution gives London vivid sunsets, full-bloomed pink and pale blue against the mud of the Thames. I stand on the hills of south-east London and watch them fade into dark.

An Argument with Myself

Narayani Menon

Once, my grandmother asked me what I was scared of – it was clear, I suppose, that something frightened me – and I said Nanny, 'I'm scared of everything.' In the twenty-five years since, I have grown up and whittled that down: now, I am not scared of everything; I am scared of most things.

I decided to explore some of my own anxieties by interviewing one of the main characters in the book that I want to write. Her name is Lakshmi, and she is, I suppose, the same age as me. We met at the Candid Arts Cafe in Angel, and she wore black jeans and a leather jacket, which she kept on, and she looked very cool. I took my shoes off and curled up awkwardly on a sofa while she looked as though she should be smoking. I immediately felt anxious.

Narayani: The title of this interview is 'On Anxiety'. Would you describe yourself as an anxious person?

Lakshmi: No, not at all.

Narayani: Wow, jealous. [*Beat*] How do you manage that?

Lakshmi: I—I think that's like saying to a person who's never broken a bone, 'How'd you manage to keep them bones together?'

Narayani: I've never broken a bone.

Lakshmi: So, Narayani, how'd you manage to keep them bones together?

Narayani: [*Laughs*] You already knew that I've never broken a bone.

Lakshmi: Did I? Is that true?

Narayani: I don't know, I invented you, so maybe you know everything about me.

Lakshmi: No, you invented me, so you know everything about me.

Narayani: I think that, because there's so much of me in you, you must know me.

Lakshmi: Is there really so much of you in me?

Narayani: I reckon so. We're both mixed-race women from London. We both tick the 26–35 box on forms. We're both often attracted to slightly pathetic men.

Lakshmi: Hah!

Narayani: It feels very good to make you laugh. It feels like an achievement.

Lakshmi: It's funny that you're anxious about interviewing me. Surely you should have the upper hand here? [*Beat*] Does it not feel like you've got the upper hand?

Narayani: No, not at all. I want to impress you.

Lakshmi: That's silly.

Narayani: Why's it silly?

Lakshmi: Because you're, like, the mother. You're the parent in this relationship. No parent has to impress their child. And you invented me!

Narayani: [*With difficulty*] I don't know if I invented you, or if I unearthed you.

Lakshmi: Either way, it makes no sense to be nervous about talking to me. [*A somewhat strained pause*] Should we get back to the interview?

Narayani: Yes. I— [*Looking at notes*] Why am I interviewing you, if you're not anxious about anything?

Lakshmi: You know the answer to that.

Narayani: Look, if we follow that logic, then there's no point in the whole of this interview and I might as well just write an essay.

Lakshmi: Perhaps you need me as an impetus to get anything done. Perhaps I help to cut through some of the embarrassment you'd feel writing this as an essay.

Narayani: Perhaps. Embarrassment is—

Lakshmi: [*Cocking her head to the side, like an expectant hunting dog*] Why are you interviewing me?

Narayani: Because we're so similar—and also because I invented you and know everything that you know—. I'm aware that you feel—a sort of—discomfort—about your racial identity.

Lakshmi: You make it sound mortifying.

Narayani: Anxiety is mortifying. It's something that you know is bad, but can't draw attention to, even though everyone's already seen it, so they know you're pretending too. It's like a permanent stain on the back of your trousers. [*Beat*] Why does your race make you anxious?

Lakshmi: Well—Growing up, I knew that my father was Irish and my mother was Indian, and I knew that I was 'half-Indian, half-Irish', and I knew, when people asked if I was half-caste, to answer, 'No, I'm mixed-race; and by the way, half-caste is a classist pejorative' with a sort of nauseating self-righteousness. But being mixed race was different to telling people that I was mixed race; it's not simply ticking a box on a form. When I was little, on holiday in India, my brother Lalit and I would tan and look—maybe not fully Indian, but not white either—and people would see us with our father and ask this white man where he had got these brown children from, because they couldn't possibly be his. I suppose I felt doubly uncomfortable: being told that I didn't look like my father's child, but also a worry in the back of my mind—did they mean it? Was he in danger of having his children taken away from him? Did he look suspect? And then in England, too, when people saw us with our mother, they would assume she was a childminder, or would treat her with suspicion, and our hackles would raise.

Narayani: I remember that, too. The other way around for me, though. I remember feeling like I passed as white and walking around London with my Indian father as a teenager, and being incredibly worried that people wouldn't be able to parse the relationship between us—

Lakshmi: Sometimes I see little kids walking around with a parent who's a different colour to them, and I wanna say hey! me too! There's an embarrassment that seems to radiate off them when their parents speak in their home language: I want to shake them and say, don't resist this!

Narayani: But you do—you do resist it. For years, as a child, I was so resistant to my name. I had all of these alter-egos—compartmentalising the different rooms in me—and even when they had unusual names, like Ariadne, they still were Western. My name was a source of shame to me, because it seemed to clash with who I was. It felt like when my mum made me wear shalwar kameez to school: I was so anxious that people would laugh at me, not because I was wearing something different, but because it'd look like I was a pretender. My name was like that too: something that might show me for what I really am, which is a shimmering mist beneath an empty signifier.

Lakshmi: Do you really think that's what you are?
Narayani: [*Furrowing brow*] I— Every time that I identify as something, as anything—as a POC, as a socialist, as an Indian, as a British person, as a queer person—I feel like if anyone lifted the lid of that signifier, they'd find an empty dustbin. I'm so anxious at the prospect of being found out.

Lakshmi: Does your name still feel like that—dangerous?

Narayani: No—now I love it. Now I cling onto it, because it's one of the few things that seems like incontrovertible evidence that I am Indian.

Lakshmi: That's a job that a second language would do, too. You don't speak Hindi, do you? Or Malayalam?

Narayani: [*Shaking her head*] I've always felt like that would have been proof to people that I wasn't white.

Lakshmi: I can do *aap ka naam kya hai.*

Narayani: I can do *behn chode* and *teri maa di pudi.*

Lakshmi: Hah! The benefits of multiculturalism, I bet.

Narayani: Totally. For years at school, I was the whitest person in my class, but we all learnt the cusses in Hindi, Bengali, Punjabi, Gujarati, Tamil. We were all polyglots when it came to profanity—and as long as I knew how to swear, no-one cared that I couldn't speak Hindi.

Lakshmi: I was so furious when I realised that other people were brought up bilingual and I was this weird shit hybrid thing, this monolingual mule.

Narayani: When you went to India, when you were little, how did your Indian family react to you?

Lakshmi: I mean, they loved me. Obviously. [*They laugh*] But perhaps they were shocked, or something on the spectrum of shock, on the way to disappointment, that I only spoke English. And I mean most of them are trilingual. Clearly, they couldn't understand why my parents would keep something as vital as language from me.

Narayani: Neither can I.

Lakshmi: There was a sort of pity when they looked at me and I think it was the first time I realised that speaking more than one language makes your brain better—I felt sort of stupid compared to them. And of course that was embarrassing.

Narayani: So you do get embarrassed about it!

Lakshmi: Yeah, I guess so, in that context. Maybe it's not embarrassment—it's quieter than that. It feels like... It's as though I'm trying to change lanes and every time I look behind me, there's a car, so I wait, and then it's not there anymore, so I check again to change lanes, but I can't, because there's a car—it's a feeling that I'm constantly wrong, and nobody knows it, but I'm only a breath away from everyone finding out. And it's physical, too; it's something that sort of roils in my belly—

Narayani: That's anxiety! You're just describing anxiety!

Lakshmi: [*Smiling wryly*] Wow. What a bummer. I guess it did make me anxious. Still makes me anxious. Being— open to other people's interpretations, being provisional.

Narayani: So you wanted to pass. You wanted to be definitive.

Lakshmi: I tried desperately to pass and was so envious of those who could, or at least those for whom their racial identity wasn't a battleground.

Narayani: Did you ever get blonde highlights?

Lakshmi: Of course I got blonde highlights! [Narayani cackles] What a nightmare. I was so determined to look less Indian, to look less ambiguous.

Narayani: Now, I feel envious of those who look more Indian than I do.

Lakshmi: Same here. And the fact that if I do present in ways that are Indian, like wearing Indian clothes or a bindi or mehndi or anything, then I look embarrassing culturally appropriative: these Indian cultural signifiers on a white girl with a tan.

Narayani: And tanning! That used to be such a battleground for me—I would sit with my Asian friends out of the sun, them because they didn't want to get 'too dark' and me because I wanted to look as white as possible, and I told people it was because I tanned so easily and didn't want different parts of my body to be different colours. I said it made different parts of my body look like parts from different bodies. A nut-brown forearm, a burnt pink shoulder, a milky breast: a Frankenstein patchwork of flesh.

Lakshmi: Hah! And what about now?

Narayani: Now I want to be the colour of an old chappal.

Lakshmi: [*Laughs*] Me too! I'm so jealous when I meet people who are half-Indian and they actually look half-Indian.
Narayani: When people say I look half-Indian, I don't really know what that means.

Lakshmi: It was strange, when I walked in and saw you, that I knew who you were, I thought, she looks half-Indian, but I was relieved, too, because you don't look more Indian than I do.

Narayani: But I'm aware of how much 'more' Indian you are than me—

Lakshmi: Only because you're making me that way. Did I always have curly hair? I don't think so. I think it used to be more like yours, lighter and straighter—

Narayani: I'm not—

Lakshmi: It feels like you're using me here to prove a point.

Narayani: I—I'm not sure—

Lakshmi: Are you making me the Indian foil to your white-passing self? Are you making me more obviously Indian because you don't feel that you can be? Are you writing me just so that I can criticise you, like when Zadie Smith wrote that anonymous scathing review of herself?

Narayani: I liked that—

Lakshmi: Yeah, but is it that you're using me as a way to escape criticism? That if I'm criticising you, then it's clear that you're not taking your privilege for granted? Is that what I'm for?

Narayani: I think that when I started writing you, I didn't realise that you'd interrogate my literary technique—

Lakshmi: It's not your literary technique I'm criticising, it's your dodgy politics; it's your use of your brownness to distance yourself from your whiteness; it's your abdication of responsibility—

Narayani: [*Panicking*] I think that's unfair—

Lakshmi: [*Abruptly*] I need a piss.

Narayani: [*Cowed*] All right.

Lakshmi didn't go to the toilet. She paid the bill and left. I waited for more than ten minutes before I went up out to the till and asked whether they'd seen her. I don't know how I feel about having been walked out on by someone I invented – a bit humiliated, I guess – but I'm glad I met her and got to talk to her. I think I feel a bit better that I was able to share the strange embarrassment of that anxiety, even if I was sharing it with myself. It made me feel less alone.

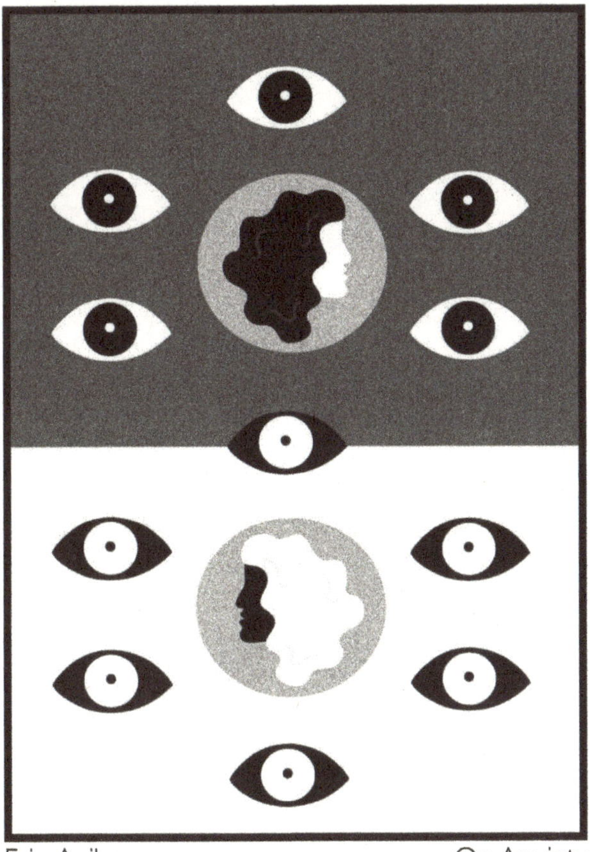

Erin Aniker On Anxiety

Stress Reduction for Companion Birds

Eli Goldstone

[Content Note: Self-harm, Compulsive Behaviour]

When I woke one morning in the house of an old friend, I was convinced that my eye was trying to force its way out of its socket. I stood in the mirror and stared, just to make sure. I woke my friend, apologetically.

'Is this really happening,' I asked.

My friend said it was not happening. The thing that I saw was not there. 'Go to sleep.'

There is something that I have learned; that lonely birds pluck their own feathers. Birds who are bored, sexually frustrated, anxious or simply seeking attention also tend to pluck their own feathers. Parrots in particular are prone to this behaviour. They are intelligent, sensitive birds, who aren't communicating when they say things that we recognise as words, but are simply repeating the sounds that they hear in the hope of being understood. They are not asking for crackers but asking to be loved and paid attention to. They are asking to be back in the jungle, where fat rain slides from the leaves of the rubber trees and where they might sleep with their heads tucked beneath their wings, their eyes gold coins dropped into the soil from above and glinting madly.

From the animal husbandry guide,
Stress Reduction for Companion Birds:
'If you must worry, do so when away from the bird.'

The anxious state tends to end my days without warning. Although I have had all day to complete the tasks that were assigned to me, the day wasn't long enough. I fall asleep and dream of hair caught in my throat, great wads of tangled hair that I pull from inside myself, wrapped around my uvula and matted in my stomach. I dream about fingernails growing from the backs and palms of my hands. I dream about electrical fires. I dream about being attacked by dogs and about people I love forcing me to swallow bottle brushes.

I try to breathe deeply but cannot. Especially in the company of another human being lying next to me. I can't fill my lungs properly. I end up hyperventilating. The person lying next to me accuses me of being too thin and of taking too-shallow breaths. I agree, but then later I think about it and become annoyed at being observed so closely and I write to that person to ask them never to contact me again. To which that person replies, 'Don't worry. I won't.'

***

The cages of beautiful birds are filled with mirrors so that they can see themselves and consider their yellow and red and green feathers and the curve of their own beaks. The people that own them want them to say particular things, but instead they repeat back the words that their owners have said to themselves without noticing. They say 'Motherfucker,' which is what I say when I have dropped something or burned myself. 'Motherfucker,' the birds say, desperately, raw pink patches on their bellies where they have pulled at their plumage as if preparing themselves to be boiled.

The anxious state is incompatible with love. Anxiety traps one inside oneself. I cannot bask in the pleasure of the other if I am so trapped, feeling every inch of skin and bone and hating it, and being confined and alone there, inside, in silence. Each finger reaching, knuckles taut, grasping for the other, for something to scratch, for something for the nails to catch on, to rip and to make sore. The body looks for something to destroy. And it finds itself.

I remember lying on the floor instead of on the bed next to the other person and being able to breathe normally, for a moment. I remember saying, 'This feels good,' and laughing. The rain began beating down outside from a cloud that had hung there all afternoon.

From the animal husbandry guide,
Stress Reduction for Companion Birds:
'Slow down, really look at your bird as if the rest of the world didn't exist and let him know that on this new day, you find him exceptional and valuable.'

The body is a prison. The body is an enemy. As if the world doesn't cause harm enough already, the body turns in on itself. It refuses food, tightens the stomach to the size of a single bullet and dries the tongue so that wine tastes sour and water tastes of pipes. I eat quickly, standing in the kitchen, trying to force down something starchy that will expand in my gut like torn notepaper, full of lines that I didn't mean to write and things I didn't mean to say.

All it takes is a hangnail. All it takes is the tiniest interruption of the skin for me to be able to take my own flesh between my fingernails or my teeth, to tear at it and make it bleed, over and over again, until my hands are pink and scarred and I cannot use fingerprint recognition on my phone because I have no fingerprints at all. 'I would make a good criminal,' I think, idly. And then I remember that I am a criminal, that I commit criminal acts all the time, in fact. Shoplifting, breaking hearts, etc.

There is a bitter-tasting spray that deters birds from self-plucking. When I was a child my mother painted it onto my nails. Of course, what good is that to me now? It isn't enough that it tastes bitter, that it is unpleasant or that it hurts. It isn't enough to stop me. It isn't the correct way to treat self-plucking behaviour in birds, either. It simply makes them sick.

Birds in captivity specifically do not like to face doorways. Anxious behaviours increase significantly in birds who are housed in proximity to, or in direct line of sight of doorways. They do not like to see people coming and going. First a person comes in with no warning. Then they remember something in another room and leave. The birds release stress hormones and they want to die.

The anxious state wants blue pills. I count my pleasures out in blue pills. When I was medicated, while walking through a certain part of Seville, I called to my companion to come and look at the most beautiful pair of shoes I had ever seen. I took them in my hands and marvelled at their oxblood leather. That was one pleasure.

Usually I am unable to pause for a moment when walking from one place to another. Usually I am breathless from hurrying. The blue pills are hard to come by. I halve and quarter them. I forbid myself from taking them on bad days in the expectation that a much worse day is likely awaiting me.

From the animal husbandry guide,
Stress Reduction for Companion Birds:
'Create rituals and predictability in every way possible. Parrots love routines because they appear to enjoy being able to anticipate what is going to happen next. In the wild, most things are predictable. The sun rises and sets without fail.'

I leave bloody thumbprints in the pages of books. I start several hundred books a year and can't finish them for some reason. I read the words with my chest tightening. I can't help but feel there is a hook in the middle of me and it is being pulled by somebody sitting in the corner of the room. How can one concentrate with all this going on? I put down the book and examine my hands for wounds that might be healing and I undo each one. I unpick each stitch that my body has had the audacity to sew.

There are so many half-read books scattered around. There are so many conversations that I have left hanging in the air. Half-smoked cigarettes. Laundry billowing like ghosts in front of the windows. There always seems to be a visitor I'm not ready for or a train that I'm about to miss. How is it that no matter how early I wake, it is always later than everyone else?

Last time I went to the dentist he informed me that I have no enamel left on my molars. He used the word bruxism. I still google this word or say it out loud from time to time. It feels good to say, onomatopoeic. I am brutish when I sleep. My jaws make a soft, crunching sound as I unconsciously devour myself.

'Perhaps I should stop sleeping altogether,' I think. But sleep is my vice. I drift in and out of sleep so easily, my brain hurrying to imagine terrible images and to show them to me.

'Oh dear,' it says. 'Look in your hand! You spat out all your teeth again.'

From the animal husbandry guide,
Stress Reduction for Companion Birds:
'If a friend visits wearing a hat that scares the bird, you must ask him to remove the hat.'

The dentist was so handsome. He was a handsome man, but he didn't offer a solution to me having no enamel left on my teeth. He simply suggested that I avoid sugar, acid, heat and cold. That I avoid things that would cause me pain. What an extremely handsome idiot.

Occasionally a raspberry seed lodges itself in one of the holes in my teeth and I dig it out with tweezers. Occasionally I use tweezers to dig into my cuticles and when I realise what I'm doing I feel ashamed. I buy sharp things and then dispose of them in the middle of the night in the kitchen bin and I stand in the electric light, alone and humming with the need to dig and scrape.

I plant things with my bare hands. I peel the labels off everything. I ruin my pans with scrubbing. I try to get to the centre of the earth by washing my face repeatedly in scalding water. I try to meditate. The meditation is not successful. Each time I recall the mantra that was given to me, I also remember the terrible advice that came with it, which was that I should try to remember there is nothing at all to be afraid of. This is nonsense, obviously. 'Still,' I think, 'it's good just to sit quietly even when one is justifiably afraid.'

Of course, the anxious state is not quiet. The anxious state is the sound of an exhaust pipe running right through the middle of my exhausted brain. That sound, that hot, violent sound, is there too when I am reading, taking a bath or reassuring a loved one that they are of consequence to the universe. 'You are significant,' I say, and the exhaust pipe clatters angrily, drowning out the sound of my voice and making me uncertain whether I have said the right thing. Making me wonder, for a second, whether I have said anything at all.

From the animal husbandry guide,
Stress Reduction for Companion Birds:
'It benefits birds greatly to get a respite from human "vibes"'.

Spinning Straw into Gold

Grace Au

'I feel like something terrible is going to happen.'

These are the words I rasp aloud to my dad when I have a panic attack while jogging along the River Tyne one frosty January morning.

I can't focus on other runners with the cars whistling on the bridge above, but I keep putting one foot in front of the other. There's just white-hot fear flooding my chest and the taste of metal in my mouth.

I've had anxiety for some time already, but it's always been triggered by something. Not this sudden searing lightning bolt of pain.

The more I think about it, it has always been present. Like a mysterious bruise blooming on a limb overnight, it was making itself known as something deeper and more volatile, ready to strike at any given moment.

***

'Another quick loss' is a phrase uttered by a psychologist a couple of years ago that has entwined itself around my brain and embedded deep roots; a spiralling pattern in my life of all carefully maintained structure collapsing, and having to recover before I can catch my breath, both exacerbating and linked to my mental health and abandonment issues. I dropped my life to move to a new city and lost the grounding holy trinity; having friends within tube-stop distance, a long-term cohabiting relationship, and cobbled-together jobs that I could actually function at. Although several of these things were slowly devouring me alive.

There's always been a sense of failure around moving back home, where the wind has teeth and the air spits salt. I am playing the part of the prodigal child perfectly, returning with no job or prospects, giving up any scrap of independence and freedom. It took two years to face the reality that being in London was destroying me. I had to come home.

Roughly six years had passed, but I was still nervous. Moving away from the North East in the first place came from a need to leave. The majority of people I grew up around were cis, straight and white. Racial microaggressions, homophobia and transphobia were brushed off as banter. I was a young person who didn't really know if I was a woman, and I knew I wasn't straight. How are you supposed to work these things out when you are young and stick out for looking a bit queer and foreign, when the queer and foreign-looking kids in the area are targeted? You escape, as many of my friends and I did.

Precious time spent discovering and celebrating my identity – in being queer, in being mixed race, in being non-binary – was being threatened by this geographical move. It was only a physical movement, but felt perilously like a step backwards.

My body started coming out in hives. I spoke about feeling isolated and trapped to my therapist. I stopped going outdoors.

***

There's only so long you can incubate. Tired of hibernating, out of desperation, I signed up for evening jewellery-making classes at the local college. A couple of years spent training, interning and working in making delicate, pretty trinkets for rich people in London had prepared me for what I'd be doing. Existing at that point was a series of lightning bolts of fear punctuated with low periods of wondering in terror when the next strike would come; I had little to lose in going to a class where the tasks would be familiar.

The room was in a small library, and very near the main exit, which my brain deemed acceptable in case I needed to blurt out that I wasn't feeling well and had to make a run for it.

Each week tiny packets of fimo clay were cut and prepared by our tutor, silver findings painstakingly counted out. Craft by numbers, almost.

I made my way to the craft section of the library, a bunting-patterned wall of shades of pink and pastels littered with titles in rounded typefaces, such as *1000 Home Projects*, *The Art of Handmade Living*, and *Tinkered Treasures*. Who even has the time and energy to complete 1000 home projects?, I think. The first week we made floating necklaces. I picked pink and white iridescent pearls. It's a safe colour scheme. I looked like a woman, picking stereotypical femme colour choices. It was fine. I was playing at being normal rather than being myself, but it was ok. No one seemed to see anything wrong with me.

The class was made up of women in their early forties to sixties. One woman said she came to classes so she got out of the house during the week, and I think about how this echoes with me. I wonder about these women. Who are they here for? I know that some people come to improve their skills for work and some are here to make new friends. Some come because it's a productive use of their free time that isn't spent caring for family. Extra-curricular emotional labour. Who am I here for? Myself? Or is this just because my therapist said it would be a good idea?

When we made things, we had to announce who the piece is for. A lot of women say their daughters, nieces, a son or a daughter-in-law. I paused before answering, 'myself'. It felt radical somehow.

I wonder if it is gendered, this intrinsic need to make things for friends and family – to provide – even in free time. How many of those pieces became peace offerings? I often think about how we manifest care in physical objects, especially women in the patriarchal caregiver role. Look at this thing I have made for you, to smooth over any bumps in the relationship we share.

As I worked, I thought of 'domestic know-how' – things our mothers, grandmothers and aunts know. Skills passed down the generations as non-binary people and women are handed the heavy mantle of homemaker. Our patriarchal society doesn't value craft seen as 'women's work', dexterity honed through years of repetition. It's easy to forget the emotional labour woven into a hand-knitted jumper, sewn into a threadbare toy or wrapped into a silver necklace in an evening class.

Knowing how to construct and make things can dissolve the magic and mystery away from the object itself. Yet in a room closed off from the rest of the library, we were weaving metal wire and beads to create beautiful objects like a coven of alchemists. We would enter the room with wire and bits and pieces, and emerge adorned in treasures.

The second week I felt frustrated. Two hours of fiddling around with some beads in a class that didn't matter but also really did because it was one of the only things that dragged me out of the flat.

The room was often hushed, simultaneously looping silver wire with the same tools in unison. The wire bit into the soft flesh of my palms, but I persevered and became calloused, until it surrendered into sloping knots and curves.

I could feel myself gradually unfurling, being able to interact with people a little more without analysing everything that they were thinking. It took time and I had to face the fear of small talk and interaction head-on. I was somehow able to do this there though. That space allowed me to begin the process of chipping away at this fear around myself. I am still learning how to be in unfamiliar spaces.

I no longer feel quite as uncomfortable just existing as myself. I felt accepted in that space, despite past experiences of existing while queer, non-binary and mixed race suggesting otherwise. Baby steps. The feeling of comfort while in a small room of strangers seemed like a foundation set, a baseline.

***

The first wire-wrapped necklace I made was from beads of my own choosing; plastic spheres painted in flame-red, white and gold. The wire structure showcases the beads so they appear to float unaided, their foundations subtler than I'd intended.

The second iteration of this design came when I braved a visit to a jewellery shop in town that sells beads, where I spotted a string of dark, coral-like cubes. The heaviness of the smooth, worn stones feels like a pendulum around my neck. The weight is not dissimilar to the swallowed-stones weight of anxiety, but instead it is strangely grounding.

It's a similar soothing effect that a heavy, carved jade rabbit that my aunt gave me as a gift years ago invokes; fashioned for nervous fingertips to wear away and smooth the edges on the delicate ears and nose deep in a pocket or palm.

No one mentions how jewellery class is a textural joy. Digging your fingertips into a box of thousands of seed beads to feel them part like a bag of grain. Rolling clay into miniscule lace doilies to gently pat onto soft marbled spheres. Holding a teardrop of translucent wave-carved sea glass in your palm until it's warm to the touch.

My mother hangs the earrings, necklaces and bracelets I've made in each class on a lamp in my bedroom like a shrine. Light glows through the glass and splashes the room in waves of red and turquoise.

At the end of the course, we gathered to admire each other's work. All around were offerings, burgundy rose petals delicately curled around a magenta heart. A hand-carved chubby jade green Buddha grinned cheekily from its wiring. Clear crackle glass beads with copper licking up the sides weaved themselves in and out of a plait. Straw has been spun into gold.

I still suffer from panic attacks, but they're more of an irritating splash rather than an enveloping wave. I sleep through the night. My therapist thinks I've done incredibly well.

The classes have ended, but I still wire wrap beads late at night in bed. It gives my anxious hands something to do. I can't say who these things are for, or if it even matters. Perhaps all that matters is translating this anxiety, this frantic motion, into beautiful objects and tasks that construct things, rather than unravel me. And that is progress, or hope.

On Making Lists
Harriet Thompson

'Come to sit on your mat with your legs crossed and your spine drawing upwards,' says the teacher.

'Take a few deep breaths here. Inhale. Let it all out with a deep exhale. Inhale. Let it out all out with a deep exhale. Bring your hands to your heart centre. I'd like you to set an intention for your practice today.'

***

You can track the chronology of your life based on the lists you have made. You learn to list numbers and the letters of the alphabet as a toddler, the names of your family members, your Christmas list, your favourite things:

Dogs
Chocolate
Drama
Playing the flute
Shopping

As you get older, you write down your homework in a list in your planner, followed by ingredients for a birthday cake recipe, then a list of items you need to pack to take on holiday. At university, you start organising your work in to-do lists so you don't forget anything:

Email lecturer about essay plan
Copy up seminar notes
Read Don Quixote

The list of books that you need to take out from the library is more than you can carry in one go.

As you enter adulthood, lists become the way you organise your life. You use them for chores, to plan your time for the day, to manage your work. Soon they creep into your thoughts, a constant stream of tasks that need completing. You try to exorcise them by writing them down, but they soon return like an irrepressible itch.

Lists can be dangerous; a constant reminder of your failure to complete things. The same tasks reappearing on the list day after day, unfulfilled. The same worries cropping up unresolved. Form an orderly line, you say to your thoughts. Join the queue, you tell your worries. You're going on the list, you inform your tasks. What's left when they've all been scribbled down? A notebook full of lists, from menial tasks to major anxieties. They sit side by side, jostling for room and attention in frantic handwriting.

***

It has been several months since you first visited the GP about your anxiety. Since then you have been signed off work for a month and quit your job, worrying about your decisions at every turn. Then one Tuesday evening you find yourself sitting in a dingy waiting room at a psychology centre. Outside, a lone saxophonist plays the theme from *The Godfather*.

There is a water cooler in the room and several *Guardian Weekend* supplements from 2016 scattered around. In the time that has elapsed since your initial referral, you have begun to wonder if you still need treatment. Things are more stable now. You are uncertain of what you will say to your therapist. You breathe heavily but not deeply. Your breaths are shallow, choking your chest. You are looking for the feeling of satisfaction that comes when you have inhaled exactly the right amount of air; the pleasurable peak before the long exhale. But it doesn't come.

You have taken to drinking water when you start to feel panicky. This usually happens on the tube, and you take small sips to calm yourself. It is a recent habit – one that your therapist will warn you is a safety behaviour you should try to avoid.

'Hello!' she says brightly. 'I'm going to get some water, would you like some?'

'No thanks,' you reply, 'I have some water in my bag.'

You realise you are smiling. When she asks how you are, you will say, 'Fine, thank you.'

The therapy room is sparse. It contains two chairs, a small table and a desk in the corner with a computer on it. On the small table between the two chairs is a box of tissues. The therapist says that today you will be looking at physical symptoms and how to deal with them.

'How does that sound?' she asks.

It's her favourite question and you always respond with, 'That sounds good.'

She is pointing at a diagram of a male anatomy annotated with anxiety symptoms. 'When we feel anxious, we often get physical sensations which come with it,' she explains. 'Do you know why we get these?'

'It's the fight or flight instinct that kicks in when we feel we are in danger,' you reply.

'Exactly,' she says. 'Whether it is real or imagined danger, our body responds the same way. So these are some of the symptoms you might experience: racing pulse, dry mouth, sweating, dizziness, nausea, muscle tension, butterflies in your stomach, shallow breathing.'

You mentally run through the list, stacking symptoms on top of each other. 'Yes, those sound familiar,' you say.

She gives you the diagram to take home.

'I'd like you to keep a journal of your physical symptoms,' she says. 'Where you are, what you're thinking about, what happens. How does that sound?'

'That sounds good,' you say.

As you lie in bed that night you make a mental list of the symptoms you feel.

Heart racing
Mouth dry
Butterflies

You wonder if you should write them down now or wait until the morning.

***

In Cognitive Behavioural Therapy you are encouraged to question yourself. 'Take that thought to court,' the worksheets tell you. Negative thinking is a common problem. As humans, we have a tendency to predict the worst. It's a kind of self-preservation which operates like the fight or flight instinct. The problem when you have anxiety is that you are using these tricks when there is no need for them. You are not in real danger.

The sessions become an endless list of words. Your therapist shows you some common types of cognitive distortions:

Catastrophising – imagining the worst thing that could happen

Fortune Telling – thinking that you can predict what will happen in the future

Mind Reading – being convinced that you know what someone else is thinking

Black-and-White Thinking – polarised thinking which places people or situations in either/or categories

'I am guilty of all of these,' you admit to your therapist as you eye the list. 'I either have to be perfect at something, or I'm a complete failure; I won't say the thing that's been bugging me because I'm certain that the other person will get cross at me; I don't want to go to the party because I know that person thinks I'm a loser.'

Reading your own thought patterns printed on a sheet of paper is both disturbing and comforting.

'Understanding that your own internal monologue can be predicted is an important step,' your therapist tells you.

You begin to catch yourself mid-flow, worrying about something until my mouth dries up and my heart races. You write the worry down. Once on paper, it doesn't feel so important. Your notebook becomes an external manifestation of your mind; a dark cave of endless lists of worries.

***

When you have finished writing your to-do list for the day, you compile another list. Then another. A list of household chores, work tasks, and worries, followed by ways to tackle the worries. You are advised to use an allotted space of time every day for worrying, so you open a new page in your notebook to make a list. But it soon spills over. You add to the list throughout the day until it becomes a teetering stack, wobbling on the page. The worry time expands.

'What about making a positive list?' a friend asks. 'Start a new notebook and every day write down five good things; things that you are grateful for; things that you are happy about. Just five things, every day.'

You find a bright red notebook which you were given for Christmas, its crisp pages blank and unlined, inviting. You take a deep breath and start the list. Finding five good things is difficult. You try to go beyond basic acknowledgements.

I ate a nice meal
I have a home
I drank a cup of tea

You know you have lots to be grateful for. You know there are countless good things in your life. But knowing that doesn't stop the fears and predictions. The positive lists soon fade out.

***

Your hands and feet are pushing into the floor, hips lifted high in the air. You drop your hips into Plank and lower down into *chataranga*.

'Move with your breath,' says the teacher.

This time, you fill your lungs and it works; the air flows without restriction. Deep breaths surge inside you, sending energy through your body. Your hands are at heart centre. Buzzing with adrenaline, you smile.

'Come back to your intention,' says the teacher.

That Moment When...

Amberin Huq

Are you good enough?
Probably not.
So you sabotage yourself...
ALEX 35
ACCOUNTANT
READING
...and him...
SIGH
ITS A MATCH
...and everything else.

and you tell yourself, better to run than let him abandon you.
you push him away just to to stay afloat.
when you become...
...a self fulfilling prophecy.
1 NEW MESSAGE

Pon Di Road

Shanicka Anderson

I come from a long line of outspoken and fearless Jamaican women. Each one just a bit bolder than the one before. Jamaica is full of bold women. There's a touch of boastfulness that comes ingrained in our DNA. Hell, our country's motto is *wi likkle but wi tallawah*. Which basically means that we are a small island, but Jamaican people are strong and mighty.

My whole life has been dominated by my festive culture. Jamaicans are known as being over-the-top and boisterous. We do not simply have parties. No, we throw bashments. Even when a loved one dies, we take our grief to the kitchens. We cook enough food and buy enough rum in order to make sure the festivities to remember our dead are spread out across nine nights.

Most of the time I spent with my extended family during my childhood was at a similar party or special gathering. And like many families during the 1990s, mine chose to video these moments. These parties have a timeless home on VHS tapes so old the footage is now grainy and full of static.

On these tapes, my cousins are usually in a circle in the middle of the party doing the bogle, the butterfly or whatever dance was popular at the time. I, on the other hand, was almost always off in a corner looking on. I shied away from the attention and wanted nothing to do with the spotlight.

Most young children lack the awareness to be self-conscious so early. But, in terms of my neurosis, I was an early bloomer. Even at a party full of my family members, I stood back too overwhelmed to join in.

In adulthood, I am a lot like that child. I learned the name for those overwhelming feelings eventually. Anxiety. It's hard to explain it to someone who does not experience it on daily basis.

Believe me, I've tried.

I sat my mother down once to explain.

'Wha' yuh nervous fa? Me nuh understand it,' was her response.

When someone has lived her entire life feeling in control and completely sure of herself like my mother has, it's difficult to imagine a person who does not.

The conversation didn't go any better when I sat down with my grandma to talk about my anxiety's physical manifestations.

'Ah juss likkle bitta gas. Drink sum tea.'

Convincing my Jamaican family that my 'invisible' illness exists is a task in itself. Convincing them that I have the illness has always felt like an insurmountable feat.

This schism between my cultural self and my mental self always seems to grow during the summer months. It's during this time that my anxiety makes it impossible for me to take part in one of the most significant Caribbean traditions.

New York summers are hot, sticky and, depending on who you ask, miserable. But I love the summer. After a long and bitter winter, the sun and warmth re-energises me. I also love the summer because it means outdoor events, parties, and, of course, Carnival.

I haven't attended Carnival since I was really young. We would go up to Eastern Parkway in Brooklyn every year and I loved it. It was sensory overload in the best way possible: the sea of West Indian flags proudly tied around belt loops or tucked into back pockets; the floats that drove past with steel drummers riding along the flatbed; and the smoky scents of jerk chicken and roasted corn that pumped out of barrel grills. Most notable were the parade dancers themselves, all clad in brightly coloured and intricately designed costumes that were complete with matching feather headdresses.

Since then my love of Carnival has only grown. I adore how carefree it is. A woman marching in costume, or *playing mas* as it is called , and dancing along to soca and dancehall is an act of reclamation and rebellion. She is exerting ownership over her body in the most traditionally West Indian way. I admire it and I envy it.

Now, the areas surrounding the Parkway, like most of Brooklyn, have been gentrified. White hipsters have moved in, who don't appreciate West Indian culture or the sights and sounds that come with it. This influx has resulted in shorter parade routes, schedules and a heavier police presence. My family got fed up with these changes and stopped attending years ago. I like to tell myself it's the reason that I've stopped going as well. But, I know it's not the truth.

The truth is, I'm terrified.

The mere thought of that many people in one place, that many eyes on me, scares me. It sets off a wave of goosebumps across my skin and forces my breathing to become laboured and staccato.

The carefree nature of Carnival is something I have yet to experience in my adult years because my anxiety takes a mental and psychological hold on me every single time.

It's hard not to feel that because of this, two separate versions of me exists. There's the adult who loves her culture and tries to be as unabashedly Jamaican as possible. And then there's the anxious little girl who still seeks refuge in dark corners, afraid to go to parties, Carnival or to receive any extra attention. Every day is a step towards reconciling these parts of me that are seemingly at odds.

This is a gradual process that looks differently depending on the day. Sometimes it looks like me missing out on another party or night out and lamenting my apparent lack of progress. But on other days, like a weekend this past summer, it looked like me throwing my own *bashment* party, with a short guest list and a playlist full of my favourite songs. I found myself swaying to the music, dancing at a party for the first time in years.

In the battle between my mental health and the expression of my culture, *whinin' up my waist* becomes equal parts self-care and recovery.

(F)logging On: Anxiety and Social Media

Sharlene Teo

Social media is a convenience that regularly makes me feel bad about myself. It incites feelings of murky, masturbatory guilt in me. When I'm feeling my worst or simply bored sometimes, I get dragged into 'compare and despair', sucked into envy/hate-scrolling vortexes three-years deep into the feeds of photogenic vacationers, productivity braggers, speculative love interests of exes I'm not even interested in and certain types of selfie-takers who get my goat. It's neither a rational nor a fair rubric, who or what I find amazing/irritating/a turn-on/a turn-off, it's just snap preference, a click-reflex. Whatever content is publicly available is laid out there for judgement and criticism. We live in a now that enables us to like or dislike someone based on their angled face, emoji curation or the way they type.

Ironically social media, with its ample scope for self-expression, also gives us the means to reduce individuals into stereotypes. I have warm and cold feelings towards people I've never even met. I've bonded and squabbled with strangers aggregated as filtered faces and named lines of text. I've largely made up my mind that I adore certain internet people, or loathe others, often with a vividness and conviction that feels personal. In fairness, I too am held to account and judged by my pictures and words. I often feel unfunny, unattractive and stupid online.

***

Writing about the internet makes me feel like an anxious little asshole. It's like describing how I chew or breathe. I write fiction for a living. But unlike fiction, which to me is all about empathising with characters, getting out of my own headspace and developing some sort of argument or through line in a story that conveys something genuine about the world, social media is all about the projection of the self, the self as sole character, the self assuming the impossible role of both public and authentic entity. You won't have an editor nicely tell you: leave those parts out, or asking what do you mean here? I feel like I have no narrative distance from the internet, and it seems both exposing and hypocritical expressing my unease with something I use unquestioningly almost all my waking day. Complaining about social media in some respects makes me feel no different to one of those endlessly baffling, mysterious specimens: the Guardian commenters who carp about anything and everything through a distinctly hoity-toity, po-faced lens; both participants and perpetuators of a toxic cycle of negativity and discontent.

Where does the line between self-care and self-indulgence lie? I only know I've crossed it when my vision blurs from having read too many think pieces about think pieces and combing ASOS for a life-enhancing coat I'll probably never find. Where is the line between narcissism and healthy self-worth? How do I know when I'm relaxing for my sanity and when I'm just idling? Right now, I have eighteen tabs open on my browser ('research'/newspaper article/celebrity gossip article/'social media anxiety'/google search/25 cute nail ideas for summer/bell hooks essay left open indefinitely but still unread etc) and I am streaming my Spotify Discover Weekly playlist which ranges from spot-on to slightly insulting. I check Twitter, glazing over the timeline and wondering how many think pieces have been written where someone describes flicking through feeds, feeling increasingly inadequate and inchoate; self-awareness a stand-in for having something more substantial to say.

To me, successful (by which I mean popularly and readily shared or engaged with) social media involves parlaying thoughts into a form of relatable, pithy half-honesty. Mary Gaitskill refers to Facebook chat, texting and tweeting as 'a hyperartificial, hive-minded way of relating', juggling clarity and frankness with a measure of witty composure and sardonic distance. At the time of writing (late summer 2017) there is a popular kind of self-ironising Twitter tone: Juno crossed with Daria crossed with Wednesday Addams. In the UK, people on Twitter address each other as 'lads' to convey, presumably, a sense of cavalier camaraderie. I'm not standing back here observing from a position of arrogant detachment; rather, this is a party I don't feel invited to. Not everyone has the knack to sound like that; I certainly don't. If I could, I probably would.

I want, casually and profoundly, to be liked. I find it so hard to read social cues online. I make missteps all the time. Within the wide sphere of people I superficially follow and people I know a little more deeply, there is a wrong and right way to bare and share parts of your life; unspoken, informal codes that shift and slip rapidly. I feel like there's some joke I'm neither in on nor understand most of the time.

***

Earlier this year, just after my violently hedonistic thirtieth birthday, I got a bout of laryngitis that rendered me mute for two and a half weeks. That is a long time for a nervous prattler like me. I was told whispering would be worse for my vocal chords than not talking at all and I found this enforced silence challenging. It made me aware of how much I use my literal voice to be listened to and understood. I communicated using the classic notebook and pen (text-to-speech apps were surprisingly unhelpful, although momentarily amusing), and checked Instagram and Twitter compulsively in an effort to remain conversant with 'the world'. Unsurprisingly, it made me feel worse. Entering into a new decade of life, I felt this Edvard Munchean silent-scream slide away from 'getting' technology and online communication intuitively, to being bamboozled by the myriad mutations of apps and my relative social ineptitude with them. The internet moves so quickly; this essay will date in the blink of an eye. How long before I start reminiscing about Instagram with the same misty-eyed nostalgia I have for MSN and Blackberry Messenger and the height of Hotmail?

***

As a teenager in Singapore in the early to mid-2000s, I loved LiveJournal. It's all but defunct now, except in Russia. The internet felt smaller and more manageable to me then, like a city you could explore on foot. LiveJournal as a platform for me was more introspective than the ballsy self-awareness of Twitter or a Facebook status: it was about confiding in a few, rather than reaching as many people as possible. My friends from junior college and I posted song lyrics and rambling ruminations, short stories and poems. You could put down what song you were listening to, maybe a mood. Our entries read like wistful letters. We'd reply in the comments.

On LiveJournal, we represented ourselves with avatars of famous people or personalities, frequently taken from film stills or animations. You'd see a Chihiro or Audrey Hepburn, Margot Tenenbaum or Frida Kahlo or a smoking Su Li-zhen or Marla Singer interacting in long, staggered threads. Nobody used their real faces, and this gave our interactions an element of play, of fantasy, almost. It was easier to say what you meant in as pretentious or fanciful a way as you wanted without being open to the criticism for it that we are today. The medium seemed more conducive to such experimentation and elaborate open-heartedness, without the instant condemnation of self-indulgence. (Which admittedly, it was.) In addition to this, we also wrote long, pensive emails to each other. So we were quixotic sad teenage girls, twee as fuck, cringingly sincere. Well, it was nice.

I kept two LiveJournals: one for personal missives, another for fiction. The personal one, when I went back to check, has since been PURGED as it hadn't been updated for such a long time. The fiction one inexplicably still exists, but it's so embarrassing I can barely browse it. Lines of code make up this dusty mausoleum of half-baked writing and fey musings, but looking at the outdated interface and my friend's old usernames, I remember how calm and safe I felt posting things during that period. I sound nostalgic, I'm aware of that, but I had a different relationship with social media then: it was an apolitical, anodyne comfort, just a way of getting my writing out there, there was a kind thrill to hitting the word PUBLISH, it was a quiet way of connecting with friends.

Nowadays I'm a lot less relaxed about it, partly because I'm on the internet all the time for work. Having some degree of control with privacy settings and contents helps to alleviate my anxiety and envy and annoyance levels. My Facebook feed, for example, consists almost entirely of dogs and dog memes from various dog appreciation groups I have joined, having hidden almost everyone else; through Twitter I've met some wonderful people and have also had some creative opportunities arise – I can't complain that the anxieties outweigh the benefits of connectivity. On Instagram I pepper the pictures of people/strangers I like with fawning, 'Embarrassing Aunt' comments. But Instagram stories has also presented me with the very contemporary feel-stab of seeing a boy I was once slightly in love with on holiday in real time with his lissome new girlfriend.

Last month, I was waiting for a bus and scrolling through all the well-lit life I was missing out on. Someone poked me on the shoulder. I took off my headphones and looked up. Two men stood before me: a policeman, and a man in his early twenties, who was blind. The policeman asked me to help the man look out for his bus. I put my phone away and made idle conversation until his bus arrived. I am ashamed to admit that was one of the first times it struck me that the comforting/masochistic dichotomy of Instagram envy was couched in a privilege I took for granted: my status as a sighted person. A 2014 study that Facebook undertook with Cornell University revealed that Facebook users with visual impairments liked and commented on photos as much as sighted people, although the former group created and shared less photos than the latter. We all have the same strong desire to engage and connect. Yet it bears remembering that the visually impaired have their own particular set of anxieties around the internet: app updates might not immediately follow accessibility guidelines, and screen readers might not be able to open certain image files or PDFs, to name just two issues of many.

***

Why do I care how strangers or a loosely defined group of people I am personally or professionally connected with perceive me? Because I often feel lonely, in the way that Michael Harris defines it, as 'failed solitude', an unproductive discomfiture wracked with self-loathing and the fear of missing out; because I want my existence to be acknowledged, even celebrated (my inner child who craves a surprise birthday party); because personal branding (shudder) is conflated with identity and cultural capital; because of sheer insecurity, and also as a form of anxious procrastination. Sometimes it's easier to project my worry and paranoia on to the outer world, as a means of avoiding work and even more uncomfortable, insular interrogations. If social media affects my mental health, surely the sensible thing is to become a Luddite?

Sure! That's like telling someone if they want to be healthier, they should cut out sugar, caffeine and booze, live on wholegrains and exercise moderately-to-vigorously five times a week – general, practical advice that is patronising at best, flagrantly unhelpful at worst. It presumes machine willpower and dismisses how tightly our sometimes deliberate, sometimes reflexive, oftentimes masochistic and pernicious habits are wound up with the daily rituals that soothe us. I cultivate very human spirals of behavior (clicking, shopping, seething, stalling) to calm myself, but that doesn't mean these patterns are healthy or wholesome. I know that. And yet I'll still keep going; idiot, wanting, wanton, and in this respect, there is no prescriptively right or wrong way to live, online or offline. This grudgingly dependent relationship I have with the internet, and how I perceive and receive people on it, is not uncommon. I still haven't figured out a foolproof way to manage the anxiety it sometimes incites in me. I guess that day-to-day the thing is to try to be more forgiving of myself, and others. Whether envy-basking in someone else's internet starriness or wallowing in squalid self-loathing, we're all just humans after all, blood and brains and feelings, shifting through screens.

Erin Aniker Millenial Angst

Certain Calamity

Lori England

It was there from the get-go;
sucked down with the last of
the gas and air and spat back
into the airless rooms of 3am feeds

every 30 minutes, I surfaced
gasping for breath like a woman
half drowned – ear cocked for the
small snuffling sounds that mean

she is snuggled safe – a pearl of a girl –
at the centre of her cellular blanket;
that her chest still rises, rolling
on the crest of an unstoppable wave.

My newly-minted superpower
is that I can see each potential
catastrophe unfolding before me;
a superspeed fastforwarding flash-forward.

The milk-scented jewel of her
breath against my cheek
seemed to signal – she is precious
so calamity is certain.

They told me it was normal to worry more
but sat teeth-chattering on my bedroom
floor, I cradled her fuzzy, sleeping
head in the crook of my arm, wishing

that I couldn't see the shape of
a thousand ways her soft certainty
could be crushed – terrified my thoughts
would conjure these breath-stealing monsters.

Lori England

Before, the image I had of this kind of thing
was of a slow sourness – a gap
left by freshly pulled teeth, a
numb space to tongue) –

not excess love, brought to the boil
bubbling over until it crystallised –
sharp and sweet like her night-cries;
its edges bloodying my gums.

What Uses of Flowers

Deborah Frempong

At ten years old, I remember telling my mother that I wanted to be a choreographer. I had been dancing in my church dance group since the age of six, and had found nothing more exhilarating than being on stage. I loved it all: the long, gruelling practice sessions on sweltering, humid Saturday afternoons, the way the dance sequences eased into my bones after I practised them a hundred times over, and then the electrifying buzz of Children's Day Sundays, when we would showcase weeks and weeks of dedicated practice. We wore our new dresses to church, bought from the boutiques weeks before. Bright and eager children, with red, yellow and blue ribbons in our twisted hair, we were excited to change out of our new Christmas attire and into our prized dance outfits.

My mother sensibly, and kindly, said to me, 'That is nice, but you know, you need to pick a career you can actually follow in Ghana, so you can do your dance on the side.' Up until then, I had no idea that one could not dance and live. All I knew was that I had incredible teachers who loved their work and taught us diligently and with grace, every week.

***

The summer of 2014, after my junior year, was the most crucial time for finding the right internship that would help propel me into The Career™ I wanted. I wanted many things. I had spent the semester studying abroad in Brazil, and by the time I returned, it was too late to find a long-term summer internship. Instead, I applied for a creative non-fiction writing workshop that would take me to Entebbe in Uganda, where I experienced some of the tenderest days of my life. It was the first time I had shared a space with so many African women collectively working on creative projects, and I had been so thirsty for such community after three years in California. My subject matter, the use of Twi in my stories and my colloquialisms made me feel like the odd one out in my creative writing classes in college, but in Entebbe I felt legible. I could call myself a 'writer', not because I had been published or because I was known, but simply because I wrote. I returned to Accra with a renewed sense of self, and decided to spend the rest of the time working on my music. In a diary entry, I recorded, 'Everything feels possible here.'

Once in Accra, I would wake up early in the mornings and take a taxi all the way from my home in Ashaley Botwe to Labadi, where I worked with a guitarist and another singer. Transportation was always a problem, and obligations to my parents, who did not take my engagements with music seriously at the time, made it difficult for me to be fully immersed in the practice. I was constantly on edge, mostly because I could not map out an end goal for what I wanted to do. My visions for any kind of longevity were stunted by an inability to envision a future that could be remotely workable. Distracted by the excitement of being home, and exhausted by the many skeptical conversations and arguments I had with my parents, I was unable to commit fully to the project and accomplished very little. At the end of the summer, I left Accra feeling like a half-baked something – an almost who was not sure what full would ever feel like.

I arrived back at school knowing I did not have any landmark internships to talk about. During the school year itself, I struggled to find time to write due to internships, campus organising and thesis research. The confidence I wore gently around my shoulders after the summer began to wear, and I started to feel incredibly conflicted about my next steps. If I cared so much about the world, if I wanted to do something with all the opportunities I had been given, what could I do? Was wanting to be a musician enough? Was it selfish? Maybe a writer, since writers seemed to be more 'useful' in public life, with their roles as social commentators, thinkers and critics? Or was I supposed to work in a non-profit? Dedicate my life to writing letters to donors or providing the direct services that were so desperately needed? Amidst all this agonising, I realised that while I felt drawn to all of these prospects, I felt less able to commit to art in particular. Although I could speak ardently about the life-saving work that art did, I found it difficult to explain why I, specifically, should be able to partake in its creative rituals. Art for art's sake was selfish, and that was the last thing I could be.

***

And so this is the mantra: have a regular 9 to 5 that pays the bills, that is tangible and legible, and work on your writing in the nights. When you get home from work, fatigued but eager, sit at your desk and then write a song, a poem or attempt to piece together a project. Perhaps, draw on the weighty romanticisation of art and the endless barrage of advice: Let the art consume you. You cannot be halfway in or out. Let the work carry you forth. Commit to it. Let it spill forth. Just write. Write every day. Write about things you know. Don't write about things you know. If platitudes work, give them a try. Remember that Toni Morrison wrote while working as an editor with three children, that Adichie was formerly in medical school; in the midst of all this, you happen to remember the others, too. Your ex-lover who dropped out of school to pursue music full time, your mentor who quit her lucrative job in architecture to become a writer. Pause when you realise that everyone is different, and that there is no formula.

I know that this has worked for several people. I also know I am afraid that giving only bits and pieces of myself to work that I care so passionately about will leave me with nothing. Like a lover who tries too hard in all the wrong ways, I will be left high-strung and dry. I remember that half-baked feeling, and know that I never want to feel that way again. In navigating my twenties – a time where we are expected to build our careers and dreams, I feel a quiet fear that nothing I do will ever be enough. Perhaps against my better judgement, and inundated with both Christian and social justice appeals – both of which rely on heightened existential and political visions of life to 'the greater good' – I find myself thinking that my art is unimportant, alongside the supposedly more important work of politics or policy. It is as though I have to choose between myself and the world, knowing, of course, that the world will move on without me. How will I balance all these things and do them well? What makes these decisions even more tenuous, of course, is that these fields are not entirely separate from each other. Art has a place in social movements, and is an indomitable world all on its own; it moves us and tears down walls. It speaks to say what no one can, as does music, as does political activism.

Despite everything I have been told about piecing together my passions into a workable tapestry, I cannot help but feel that something will have to give. The stage, with all its revelatory lights, will break and my ink will run dry.

***

Inundated by all these thoughts, a singular truth rings through my head that the ability to ponder over career paths is by all means a privilege. In Ghana, only about 13 per cent of women and 19 per cent of men continue their education up until the tertiary level, or much less have the option to pursue all the types of careers they want. Access to quality education is so arduous that many students drop off along the way and even those who finally get their degrees experience the job market's relentless ability to shut them out. Considering our social and economic realities, the idea that art should be treated as a hobby is something we do not only know intimately, but believe. In a country where cultural and artistic institutions are simultaneously neglected and exploited, parents frequently stifle the artistic pursuits of their children in order to move them towards more 'sustainable' careers. The people who end up in the arts are regarded as lucky one-offs, misfits and non-conformists; their world is unstable, something that thrives in spite of.

Children of middle- and upper-middle-class families, especially, are discouraged from entering the popular arts industries in favour of white-collar jobs that will confer the social status that maintains a life of comfort. Knowing this, I feel the creeping guilt that descends and wraps itself around my head, so I am unable to create freely.

***

In my first year of graduate school, when I begin to struggle under the weight of rent payments and increasing workloads, my commitment to my creative work suffers. I find it difficult to do what I truly love: to write or sing. It is hard not to blame myself for choosing a life that makes it difficult to do art. Everything suggests that it is because I am lazy, not ready to commit, and that I do not want it badly enough. I tell myself that I will fail, not that I am overwhelmed and that it is ok to rest. One night, I am speaking to my high school English teacher on Facebook. I have just shared with him a presentation I gave on colonial identity, with focus on Ousmane Sembène's *Black Girl* and Ferdinand Oyono's *Houseboy*, a text he first taught me. He tells me how proud he is of me, and as the conversation goes on he interjects, 'On a lighter note, have you abandoned singing? You were so good.'

I am taken aback for a moment by this innocent, kind enquiry and I am unsure of how to reply. It is a dormant memory, in the way one remembers the pain of a body part that aches only when touched. Against the harsh glare of my computer screen, I feel the sinking feeling of incompleteness build up again. I reply to say something about being busy and not having time. It is truthful, yet I feel like a liar.

On nights when the anxiety hits, I watch TV and try to mute all the thoughts that roam freely and comfortably set up shop in my head. The cult of productivity – of working 9 to 5 while writing the next biggest novel, or being a broke graduate student while self-publishing your first book – is too much for me. I try to remind myself that I am not superhuman, that everything will be OK, that the crushing news all over Twitter and Facebook and my inability to write for three weeks will soon pass. I mourn for Accra and Lomé and Charleston. I volunteer. I donate to feminist organisations when I can. On other nights, I try to draw a map of what is possible in my lifetime, I make a list of artists who lived as bakers and doctors and teachers and singers. I devise timelines and deadlines, a string of meditations that might help me hold onto the pathways of possibility and devotion. I call it spirit-work, invoke Audre Lorde and Mercy Oduyoye, and fight all my inner feelings until I lay on my bed, exhausted.

I tell myself I am only having a bad night, a bad week, a bad couple of months. I rage about not being able to be five dynamic people at once. I weep because I am terrified of regretting everything.

***

Most of the time the question revolves around the freedom to do art: what it would look like for parents and guardians to accept it as a valid path, what it would look like for artists to live well, pay their bills and thrive off their work. The question that rests with trepidation, and on the edge of my tongue, however, is what the freedom to do it all looks like. It feels obnoxious to say, but what I want is to live fully, and to be versatile with all the gifts and talents that I have been so graciously given; gifts that in return, give me life. I desire to do work that is meaningful, work that may disrupt, even if in the tiniest possible way, an unequal and cruel world. Work that is permissible in all its forms.

When I read Ken Saro-Wiwa's writing in particular, I feel the weight of every word, every syllable and every phrase that tries to expose the perfidies of death. The summer I visited Uganda, I read his books on all my flights and sighed at the buoyancy of each old, corroding page that belied the heaviness and timelessness of their content: the people of Ogoni still suffer the same struggles for which he would die so unjustly. As I read his work, my sensibilities around art and how to do good within the world revolve around each other, tugging at something in me that is fused and will never dissolve.

Similarly, Lorraine Hansberry teaches me something about the way we think about art, and about how to dutifully destratify what we consider characteristic of meaningful, useful living. In one of her last works, *What Use Are Flowers?*, English professor Charles Lewis Lawson, a hermit who decides to abandon the world, emerges to find it in a post-apocalyptic stupor, with all of humanity destroyed, save for nine scraggly children who have no inkling of socialisation. They are, in Charles's mind, savages, and he begins to show them the ways of the world, teaching them to speak English, wear clothing, but most importantly, about the uses of things. When he tries to teach the children about intangible things, like love and beauty and flowers, the keen students ask him, 'use?' For a newly constructed world that has revolved around the importance of things, as well as the stark productivity that is required of living, these wide-eyed children are right in categorising according to functionality. About flowers, Charles explains,

'One may smell them
One may touch their petals and feel heaven
One may write charming verses about them'

And about music, he says, 'YOU JUST SING!'

Before he finally passes on, Charles, in an attempt to teach his namesake, a child he has named Charlie, something about the endless vortex of life and death, whispers,

'Use ... What use? Charlie, the uses of flowers were infinite...'

Through the children, we experience the sheer bewilderment of how to conceptualise those things for which we are unable to make useful in the ways we would want, but that are crucially important to how we live in this world, how we love, how we give. The children, more so than Charles, are my guiding light, because they teach me to trouble my knowledge and to see sight itself as both deceptive and illuminating. They help me remember that my anxiety will appear to me in different forms, in love, ego and fear, and that it is my job to parse out which forms I will attend to. I hope to always choose love.

And so I turn the phrase 'what use are flowers?' over and over again in my mouth, let it carpet the insides of my chest and trace along the curves of my palms. It becomes a protector, a soft shield on the days I am unable to see past the fog of uncertainty. To say that I have deciphered how to navigate all my desires would be a dishonest telling; instead I have tried to think about all my pathways – the ones that are wonderfully ignited and kind, where I feel like the spritely little girl doing what she was meant to do, and those that weigh heavily on me – as inevitable. I manage my fears, remind myself that the world needs all I can give in equal measure, and that I also, need what I can give. I strive for the moments when I can see each doing, despite its assigned metric of usage or relevance, for what it is – infinite.

The Alligator

Alice Slater

[Content Note: Self-harm, Suicide, Child Abuse]

Just as I'm falling asleep, a set of high beams sweep an arc across my bedroom ceiling and I'm jolted by an uncontrollable sense of panic. The back of my throat burns and intrusive thoughts of dark car parks, of strangers, of unspecified violence clatter for my attention. I switch on the Himalayan salt lamp by my bed, sink into the rose-gold gloom and wait for the wave of fear to wane. At least, for now, I'm alone.

This growing sense of dread could be related to a couple of things but I can't be sure. They might be the cause of the dread, but they might also just be symptoms. I have a lot of symptoms.

Firstly, this week is Pancake Day in England, which means it's Mardi Gras in New Orleans. I try to avoid thinking about that, but some thoughts are like gas and expand to fill all available headspace.

Secondly, I realised today that it's been three weeks since I had the nerve to open my front door. I used to try to open the front door at least once a day, even if I didn't have an online shop due. Just to check for junk mail stuffed under the doormat, or to look at the birds pecking for seed-scraps in the front garden, or even just to feel fresh air on my face and remind myself that the world extends beyond my curtains. I guess I fell out of the habit.

Finally, I suppose more prominently, my alligator came back. It felt like a flashback or a dream, or a flashback of a dream, but I'm pretty sure I was awake the whole time. I was making a cup of peppermint tea and, quite out of nowhere, I felt that it was behind me, stretched out across the sink and draining board with its avocado-skinned tail grazing the lino floor.

When the kettle boiled, I filled the mug with hot water and I walked into the bathroom without so much as a glance at the kitchen sink. I locked the door, dropped to my knees and closed my eyes. I could hear the faintest of knocks on the bathroom door: knock kn-kn-kn knock knock. The morning sun was weak and the glass of the small window was laced with frost. I wanted to open it, to let the fresh cold air leak into the tiny room and strip away the harsh smell of cleaning fluid and bleach, but I couldn't move until I felt safe again, and by then my tea had grown quite cold.

***

In New Orleans, there is a big party in the street instead of Pancake Day. The man with the chewing tobacco tells you it is called Mardi Gras, which means Fat Tuesday in French. That sounds made up but then Carla says that Mardi Gras is made up, and Pancake Day is made up and so is Christmas and Halloween and everything was made up by someone at some point.

You ask her if Bonfire Night is made up and she pauses as she unwraps her new pack of cigarettes and says she guesses so because it was never really about fireworks or Hook-a-Duck until later but it was really based on something that happened a long time ago and you say, Yes Guy Fawkes, and she says, Yes, exactly and you say, Well in that case Christmas is real then because it's based on Baby Jesus.

The man with the chewing tobacco spits brown goop into his paper cup. He has rough-looking hands with cracked palms and he sits outside a shop filled with things like fridge magnets and t-shirts that say NOLA and NEW ORLEANS and CRESCENT CITY and WHO DAT and SAINTS in big colourful purple and green and gold letters.

--Well now Mardi Gras's the day before Lent. Folks need to let loose before forty days of fasting, he says to you as Carla pushes her change into the watch pocket of her denim shorts.

--My Nan always makes me give something up for Lent, you tell him. Last year I gave up ketchup.

The man with the chewing tobacco does a hearty chuckle and you see his teeth are stained brown and ugly like woodchips in the playground near your house in Northampton. He reminds you of the man your Nan buys her fruit and veg from, but instead of smoking a rolled-up cigarette he chews it like gum.

Carla blows smoke into the air between you and says OK see you later to the man with the chewing tobacco and starts walking away without you and your sandals slap against the cracked pavement as you hurry to keep up.

--Make sure your mama gets you a slice of King Cake, honey! he calls after you and you wave over your shoulder because you think that sounds like a really good piece of advice.

***

My alligator usually visits me in the night. Just as I begin to drift to sleep, I feel it shift its weight or swish its tail and the air changes. Sometimes, it basks on top of my wardrobe and sometimes it's stretched across the bedroom floor, curling and uncurling its tail against the rug. Sometimes I can't see it at all and that's what frightens me the most because I can still sense it. I suspect in those moments it drifts in the shallows underneath my bed. That's the worst because then I can't bring myself to put my feet on the floor in the morning. I've been trapped there for hours daring myself to just do it, but then before I drum up the nerve to let it have me I feel the air change and I know it's gone.

I last left the house in January to buy grape juice, razor blades and tampons. I used to buy my unexpected essentials from two different shops because I didn't want anyone thinking anything of me. I like to be unremarkable and even I know those are weird things to buy regularly together. I only shop in the nearest corner shop now, when I can make it out the front door, even though it's the most expensive and the brothers that take turns working behind the counter are starting to give me funny looks. My desire to get back to the safety of my flat as quickly as possible eventually overcame my desire to keep up appearances.

I do most of my shopping online so I never need to buy toilet paper or bleach or pasta or that kind of thing from the local shops. They're cheaper if you buy them in bulk anyway. I never buy razor blades online because I always tell myself I don't need them anymore. That's a total crock of shit, but here we are. It's difficult to find the specific brand of grape juice I like, but my local shop stocks it especially for me, so it's important that I keep going to buy it otherwise they might stop. It's fizzy and tastes almost plastic, like the scented rubbers school children like, but it reminds me of my mother and I have so little of her left.

***

In the morning, the neon lights of Bourbon Street shine in pastel colours against the bright sunshine. The air is filled with the smell of spilled drinks and fresh donkey dung and hot oil for frying doughnuts and oysters and crawfish, which look like tiny lobsters. Everyone calls them mud bugs, which makes them sound disgusting. Carla drinks a banana daiquiri from a styrofoam cup and you walk around shops in the Quarter that sell leather masquerade masks and Tabasco bottles the size of your thumb and strings of the jewel-coloured beads that hang from the trees and the street signs and the wrought iron fences. You collect glossy flyers for graveyard tours and ghost walks and vampire talks, and there is even a company that will take you to the swamp on a boat to see the alligators. You show it to Carla and she puts it into her handbag without even looking at it.

In a bookshop that smells of skin on paper, she buys you a glossy book about the folklore of Louisiana. The cover is the peachy colour of a mussel in its shell, and it is illustrated with a silhouette of a man playing a saxophone beneath a gas lamp whilst a couple dance on a balcony across the street. You carry the book against your chest all day, delighted by its thickness and its power and its knowledge.

When Carla finishes her drink, her breath smells like the foam bananas you get from the corner shop at home. You follow her banana breath into a cramped shop full of candles and spells, where incense smoke curls around strings of beads and dream-catchers that hang from the ceiling like the Spanish moss that hangs from the trees.

--Look, these are called altars, Carla says. There's one for the Voodoo Queen Marie Laveau, and one for her daughter. You leave an offering and in return they bring you good luck.

The altars are just old mantelpieces crammed with dust-covered trinkets; foreign coins, postcards, ticket stubs, matches, small toys, playing cards, herbs, incense, voodoo dolls, Mardi Gras beads... hundreds of random objects from hundreds of tourists' pockets. Carla reaches up to her ear, unfastens one of her silver hoops and places it neatly on the altar in a mote of dust.

--Shouldn't you leave an earring for the daughter as well? you say, pointing to the laminated signs stuck around the mirror that say NO PHOTOS and DO NOT TOUCH THE ALTARS and DO NOT REMOVE OFFERINGS and PLEASE LEAVE OFFERINGS FOR

BOTH MOTHER AND DAUGHTER.

--Mothers and daughters need different things, she says and you think, oh.

***

In the evenings, you settle into a routine. Carla leaves you alone locked in the motel room and you're not allowed to open the door unless she does her special knock which goes knock kn-kn-kn knock knock. It's really important she gets it exactly right and you have to listen really carefully to make sure it's exactly right before you open the door and that's why there's the three little half knocks in the middle. She says someone just listening casually might think it was just six quick knocks but we know to listen for the three that almost whisper to each other because those are the three that say it's fine, it's me, you can let me in.

When Carla goes out, you watch bright game shows on the fuzzy telly and eat cold Pop Tarts in strange flavours. When you realise how quiet the motel is at night, you grow bold. You go to the vending machine in the car park and drop quarters into the slot for cans of fizzy grape juice that your Nan would never let you have at home. Sometimes you try on Carla's shoes and dresses and lipstick. Sometimes you even walk out to the ice machine in the lobby just to try being a grown up for real, although the thought of being caught outside the room terrifies you and you look over your shoulder like you're afraid you're being followed even though you are not because there is never anyone else around.

You read all the flyers from the French Quarter and prepare convincing pitches such as *Hey Carla did you know that alligators show a remarkable degree of parental responsibility for reptiles and the mothers carry the babies in their mouths and build nests and guard them until they are strong enough to fend for themselves? And the babies are called hatchlings? Maybe we could go on a swamp tour and I could write my summer essay about alligators?* but when she gets home from the Quarter she just wants to sleep until noon and has no interest in your alligator facts.

When Carla told you she was going to take you to America, you thought you would be sipping frothy pink milkshakes peaked with squirty cream and driving around in a shiny peppermint open-top car and looking at the Hollywood sign, or maybe going to all the theme parks in Florida and eating churros – whatever they are – covered in cinnamon sugar. You imagined shiny shopping malls filled with pretty girls that you could copy so when you went back to school in September everyone would gather around you and ask where you got your cool pencil case, your cool skirt, your cool backpack, and you could shrug and say, Oh, my mum got it for me in America, just like Olivia Matthews does every year with her scented pens and her holographic tubes of bubblegum lip gloss.

***

My alligator is appearing more regularly. Sometimes, when I close my eyes, I feel it swim past me through the air. It has learned to swim. It couldn't do that before. I'm less safe than ever and I have no way out. Now that it can swim in the air around me, I don't understand why it hasn't taken me yet. It just watches my every move, preventing me from popping pills or cutting myself. Sometimes it even looks sad.

I don't have any friends left. I lost touch with a few people when I quit being around alcohol, and another wave when I couldn't eat in restaurants anymore. When I cut out trains and buses and my world shrank to the size of my immediate neighbourhood, pretty much everyone stopped bothering. Those who did reach out were met with a stubborn radio silence. I thought it would be easier on everyone if I just faded into the background, then I could slip away and hardly anyone would notice. That was three or so weeks ago, around the time the alligator appeared, around the time I gave up entirely on going out.

I used to imagine my life as a series of adventures sprawling ahead of me: learning to drink beer in sixth form with a bunch of arty friends who would invite me to gigs and festivals, then on to university, a leaf-strewn campus somewhere in the North. I'd wear autumnal colours and drink lattes from paper cups and talk about philosophy and politics, and I'd have a string of affairs with all sorts of interesting, beautiful people. And then, adulthood. I imagined a house in Norfolk, cats weaving figures-of-eight around my ankles as I watered plants, my home decorated with candles and books and pictures of all the places I'd been.

Things turned out differently. No college, no university, no affairs, no house in Norfolk. My life is quiet, my world is small.

***

Sometimes Carla brings you back presents from the Quarter, like strings of shiny plastic beads or crawfish sandwiches wrapped in paper or little green plastic hand grenades that smell of lime juice that you line up on the headboard of your bed. One time she comes back with little square doughnuts that shed dusty drifts of icing sugar all over the bed and even though you are mostly asleep you eat one just to show her that you always wake up when she gets home, even if she is gone all night.

Sometimes she brings friends back with her from the Quarter and when she does that you pretend to be asleep and bury your head under the covers and try to block out their slurred sloppy conversation that makes the air smell toxic like spilled nail varnish. Carla's friends are always American and they are almost always men. They leave before dawn and she always sleeps late on those days and you have to go and get your own breakfast with the dollar notes and coins left crumpled on the nightstand, mixed with all the other stuff from her pockets like matchbooks and cards from bars with phone numbers written on them in biro.

Sometimes you walk all the way to the French Quarter to visit the man with the chewing tobacco. He has baskets of dried alligator heads for sale in every single size imaginable, from teeny ones that fit in the palm of your hand to huge ones that frighten you a little bit because the teeth are so sharp and the eyes are so dead.

Sometimes you just go to the 7/11 on the corner and buy a cherry slushie that stains your spit pink and sometimes you just walk for a while and count the cracks in the pavement. You know you must be leaving soon and so you ask Carla about the swamp tour but she rolls onto her back and pulls the scratchy motel sheet over her face and says go a-way like you are the most irritating thing on the planet.

It rains and rains and rains on your last night in New Orleans and you think maybe the city is sad to see you leave because you've been here for so long you feel like you belong here. You are sad too and in your head you say goodbye to everything you walk past – Goodbye pancake house! Goodbye 7/11! Goodbye Café du Monde with your funny doughnuts and all-night coffee!

Carla makes you wear a dress and you go into the French Quarter together for dinner and she says that afterwards she will take you to a bar and you can have a sip of her most favourite drink in the whole world. She is pretty and tanned and she has her make-up done all special and it feels like a real celebration.

The rain washes all the muck from the city into the gutters and strands of stray beads glitter in the dirty puddles. Carla leads the way because she knows these streets now. She takes you to a restaurant where they always keep the same table empty with a candle burning for the bearded ghost that lives there. There is a man in a cowboy hat already sitting at your table and at first you think it's a mistake but then Carla kisses him on the cheek and you join him.

For dinner, you eat oysters on the half shell squeezed with lemon juice and then you eat a big bowl of jambalaya and then a slice of pecan pie. The man in the cowboy hat picks up the bill and Carla kisses him on the knuckles and says thank you and she really looks like she means it.

Then the three of you go into a dark bar that's thick with smoke and smells of ghosts. Candles in red jam jars flicker on spindly wooden tables and somewhere in the gloom you hear a piano play. You know you look older than twelve, at least fifteen, but America is strict and you can't sit in the bar if you're underage so Carla buys a Hand Grenade to go and gives you the little plastic hand grenade that floats in it and at last you know where she kept getting them from because you did wonder.

The Hand Grenade is like a slushie and it is bright green but it stains your spit yellow. You only drink a little bit of it but it scrunches your belly and you feel too full as you walk through the rain-damp street next to Carla, who has looped arms with the man who paid for dinner, and you ask to go home. The man in the cowboy hat points to a white pony and cart that's parked in the street and says, Wouldn't it be neat to take a pony ride together?

The pony snorts and its cream mane shivers and you so desperately want to pet its velveteen nose and ride in the cart and pretend it's the olden days, but the back of your throat is burning like you swallowed a battery and your belly hurts and you tug Carla's hand and shake your head. She tells you to grow up and says you're a big girl now and that you're going to ruin the happiest night of her life and that makes your eyes fill with tears and it's been so much fun to spend every day and every night with Carla but you're starting to get worried about what will happen when you get home, like will you be really far behind in school and will Nan still let you live with her and will Carla disappear again?

***

I often think about that trip, when I was eleven or twelve and Carla kidnapped me and took me to New Orleans. That's the last time I remember being truly happy, running around the streets of the French Quarter and collecting stray Mardi Gras beads, drinking those rainbow slushies, just being a kid. I hardly remember the details, just that I was happy and then I was not. I don't blame Carla for what she did – she had me too young, I understand that now, but some things just can't be undone.

***

The oysters and the jambalaya and the Hand Grenade and the excitement make you sick, the sickest you've ever been. You throw up all down yourself and all over the pavement in front of a bar full of blow-up tropical palm trees. Carla sluices you down with bottled water that is so cold it makes you shiver, even though the air is so warm and so still and so close it is like hot breath on your skin.

Carla takes you back to the motel in a taxi but you are sick in the car and the driver stops in front of the man with the chewing tobacco's shop and makes you both get out and he yells so much you can't help but cry as you drop onto the concrete in front of the baskets of dried alligator heads.

As Carla drags you away, the man with the chewing tobacco says, Hey honey, she all right? You need a hand? and Carla says to him, Go fuck yourself you old creep.

In the motel room, she strips you down and puts your clothes in the bathtub. You lie on your bed on the scratchy blanket and feel feverish and sick and when you wake from dreams that feel real you see that she is not there and you try to listen to her knock but there are men in the car park yelling and they frighten you, oh they frighten you so much, and what if Carla wants to get back to you but the men in the car park won't let her?

On the nightstand there is an alligator head, like the souvenirs that your friend, the man with the chewing tobacco sells. Did you see him? Did the taxi stop in front of his shop? You have echoes of an idea of what might have happened, but everything is churning like a slushie machine and you can't think straight. It stares at you and you dream some more and you think about where it came from and how it ended up on your nightstand watching an English girl sick up slimy oysters into a 7/11 carrier bag in a motel in New Orleans and you feel so sad for it, so sad for the pair of you, that you even cry a little. It looks back at you with its gaping frozen smile and you wonder if it feels even a little bit sad for you too.

***

This won't be my life for much longer. The alligator is here all the time now, constantly watching me with its blank eyes. It floats dreamily through the rooms of my flat, circling my blades and my medicine. When the sun shines, it drifts through the closed window and basks in the light. As its skin warms through, mine glows. As it breathes in the fresh air, my chest rises and falls. My alligator rolls in the air outside my window, and in those moments, my hand twitches and my mouth goes dry because only then am I free to swallow pills or use a blade without it knowing, but I can't bring myself to do myself harm when my alligator looks so free, so happy, and so at peace – so at peace – I almost feel like I could open the door and walk through it myself.

***

When you wake up you are in a hospital bed and you are alone. Your stomach, your throat, feel raw, like the sting of a skinned knee. Your head is whooshy, like the wind and rain against the window outside. You can hear a conversation through the curtains between a man and a woman and they are saying things like *no sign of the mother* and *lucky he noticed something wasn't right* and no insurance and *her grandmother is coming to get her, she's coming, she's on her way right now* and *she's just relieved that she's ok* and *even goddam gators know how to take care of their kids.*

Hangnail

Rosemary Waugh

[Content Note: Self-harm, Compulsive Behaviour, Blood]

There's blood on my skirt. I'm walking around Hyde Park with blood on my skirt. A small splattering of red splotches down the right-hand side. It's not a lot, but it's dyed an arc of magenta streaks onto the teal green fabric. Where has it come from? Nowhere more dramatic than a small open blob on the knuckle of one thumb. While I don't how it originated, I know why it's still there. It's there because I keep rubbing at it with the third finger on the same hand. Rubbing, just gently. Rubbing, so the tiny membrane of scab that periodically tries to form is always worn fresh away.

This isn't a conscious act as such – I only notice I've been doing it when I spot the embarrassing trail of sanguine blotches – and it's not normally a knuckle scab that my hands preoccupy themselves with whilst my brain is elsewhere. Normally it's that lovely line of thick skin underneath the thumbnail, a meaty strip of leather ripe for digging at until it comes away like foil from a crème brûlée pot. Alternately, it's those tantalising bits of sharp, hard skin at the edge of the nail, cracked flakes begging to be given a helping hand in their bid for separation.

I realise this is disgusting. No one likes someone who picks their own spots, bothers a scab or gnaws at worn-down fingernails. I've had this horrible nervous habit for as long as I can remember. I have vague memories of sitting in school nibbling – yes, *nibbling* – at the skin around my poor, abused thumbs. I do it almost entirely unconsciously, often between writing sentences or when I'm walking (as is the case in Hyde Park).

At the beginning of 2017, the shame of possessing such an unattractive and somehow juvenile behavioural trait got the better of me and I asked a hypnotherapist, who I was seeing for other reasons, if she could help. She told me the part of the human brain governing compulsive behaviour is like that of a young child. To help stop the behaviour, you need to treat it like the four-year-old it is. Start by being direct and determined. Each time you find yourself doing it, halt and mentally say: 'No, we do not do that any more.'

I immediately started on this very minor step of habit breaking, saying in a school ma'am voice to myself: 'No, Rosemary, we do not do that any more,' whenever I caught myself mid-skin pull. And it turned out the hypnotherapist was telling the truth. The part of the brain governing compulsive behaviour really is like a young child – just not necessarily in the way she was describing. Within a few days, my inner compulsive child had, like all pre-schoolers, found a way around the authoritative adult. I'd suppressed the urge to pick at my skin, but instead I'd started aggressively running my index finger over the surface of my thumbnail like I was trying to erase it. Less damaging, and less likely to cause bleeding, yes, but swapping one nervous hand movement for another only marginally different didn't strike me as the biggest success.

This minor but ultimately psychologically interchangeable adjustment to my behaviour led me to wonder, of all the mildly destructive compulsive behaviours a person can have, why does picking at skin so often suggests a low-bubbling anxiety? Compulsive behaviours are almost by definition meaningless; the person keeps doing them even when they don't consciously want or need to. In my case, I pick at my skin when not knowingly anxious. The behaviour actively increases when I'm exposed to stress – then I'll even return to the childhood act of softly biting at the skin – but the rest of the time I just do it because I do it. Yet dismissing the habit as meaningless is short-sighted, as surely nothing in human behaviour is a coincidence. What was lurking in my subconscious that made me start chipping away at little pieces of skin rather than, say, washing my hands or smoking? Why skin?

In *Skin: On the Cultural Border Between Self and the World*, Claudia Benthien dissects the myriad and evolving ways in which skin has been understood since the eighteenth century. Using examples from literature, art and science, she considers the skin as a site of identity, not just in terms of its colour, but also in the manner it may be tattooed, pierced, fake-tanned or stretched using cosmetic surgery. Benthien's underlying hypothesis is that the human epidermis has become 'an increasingly rigid boundary in spite of the fact that medicine has penetrated the skin and exposed the interior of the body'. In other words, scientific advancements have not prevented a paradoxical increase in assigning other meanings and significance to the collection of cells encasing the bones, organs, veins and tissues of the human body.

In the chapter 'Boundary Metaphors', Benthien discusses a selection of phrases from European languages that relate to skin and, in doing so, reveals a fundamental division in popular understandings of the substance. Many of Benthien's examples are historic or modern German expressions (the book was originally written in German, with an English-language edition translated by Thomas Dunlap). However, she also includes examples from English, French and Italian. Added to this, many of the German examples she chooses still work when translated into English. Among these figures of speech are, 'I was scared out of my skin' or 'it really got under my skin'. My personal favourite is, 'it makes my skin crawl'. The additional insect-like movement of the skin viscerally captures the feeling of deep discomfort this idiomatic phrase refers to.

Benthien, however, isn't just interested in noting this shared linguistic phenomenon in European languages. Instead, she describes how the expressions she identifies suggest two different conceptions of skin. One group hinges on 'the idea that the skin encloses the self: skin is imagined as a protective and sheltering cover but in some expressions also as a concealing and deceptive one. What is authentic lies beneath the skin, is hidden inside the body.' For example, the judgement 'she is uncomfortable in her own skin' suggests the skin is a bodily box for the self to either rattle around in or dwell at peace.

Consider how this conception of skin links to the habit of removing tiny pieces of human material. The idea that the 'real' self is hidden below the skin can easily be tallied with a belief in some version of a 'soul' – an intangible spirit-like entity that represents the essence of a human. Despite the growing number of self-identifying atheists in English-speaking countries, well-known sayings such as 'only skin deep' suggest that the idea of a more genuine version of a person residing either literally below the skin or, more vaguely, as unconnected to the corporeal being, still pervades the collective imagination.

The experience of anxiety can feel like a surplus of feelings; an overwhelming amount of emotion experienced because you are too raw, too open and too empathetic to anything bad or stressful occurring in the surrounding environment. You are like a sponge soaking up what other people are able to sail through like toy boats. If this is what it feels like to be anxious, why, in times of raised anxiety, would I decide to pick away at the one physical layer that does exist between – using the logic underpinning this group of linguistic phrases – myself and the wider world?

If anything, we tend to do the opposite in times of vulnerability and cocoon ourselves in extra layers of jumpers, coats or duvets. Every once in a while, I will conjure from my memory the sight of my grandma standing in the door of the bedroom as I tried on some of her old clothes. 'They're armour – that's what my mother would say,' she said. 'They're armour.' And I'll pull myself out of whatever place of rawness I'm in and make a real effort to encase my body in an impenetrable uniform of structural dresses, blazers and lipstick – make-up being the most literal way of adding an extra, reinforcing layer to the skin.

A brief consideration of skin-as-covering, then, doesn't immediately lend itself to explaining skin-picking as a manifestation of anxiety. If anything, it defines the action as counterproductive as a means of abating the experience. However, Benthien does explore a second group of skin-related phrases. This other 'group of sayings equates the skin with the subject, the person: here the essence does not lie beneath the skin, hidden inside. Rather it is in the skin itself, which stands metonymically for the whole human being' (though over the last two centuries, Benthien notes, German expressions that fit into this second category have become scarce). One example still in use in English is 'she saved my skin'. These phrases essentially view the skin as representative of the whole person and provide a more potent possibility for explaining my bad habit. If the skin is, quite literally, 'you' then wanting to destroy it in times of stress is easier to grasp.

A few weeks back, I started explaining this essay to a friend who said, with a kind pointedness, 'it could just be considered self-harm.'

And I realised, yet again, that I might well be trying to talk/write my way around confronting the fact that this is almost certainly an unhealthy habit to have and one I should make a concerted effort to address. I even wonder if writing this essay has been another attempt by the inner four-year-old to avoid the difficult job of quitting. Writing this has given me a great excuse not to. I told myself it would add a falseness to the piece if I was 'cured' before writing it, so I stalled trying to quit. If the skin is the self, then slowly destroying it by digging away at the edges when you're anxious has a certain logic to it. It's like acting out the desire to evaporate at peak moments of stress or, as people often say, 'I wish the ground would swallow me up'. I wish I could just disappear.

Bulking up the skin by adding extra layers to it – be it in the form of clothes, make-up, tattoos or other adornments – hints at a desire to hide the self from the world. Yet I can think of one example where strengthening and expanding the surface of skin is better understood through the lens of the skin-as-self. The artworks of Lucian Freud are full of skin. Almost without exception, his models are white and he painted their skin using a particular brand of white paint, Cremnitz White, that added a visceral density thanks to the lead in the paint.

In 2012, I visited the major retrospective of Freud's paintings at the National Portrait Gallery. With reproductions it is hard to fully appreciate the thickness of the layers of paint, instead the works appear more blotchy. But see them in a gallery, and the expanse of skin is overwhelming. Rather than create a sense of concealment, the denseness of the skin suggests an intensifying of the subjects' humanity. The people in the paintings are so intensely human – monuments of unique flesh; bodies that deserve repeat observation. Until this point, I knew little about the artist except that his nudes were often considered 'cruel' in their hyper-realisation of human flesh. A mean-spirited view of his subjects, however, was not something I sensed when looking at the pictures. Walking around the exhibition, I kept thinking that the portraits should be considered anti-war paintings. Studying the tender, tactile skin depicted makes it impossible to fathom how someone could deliberately destroy it. Or how another human could rip it apart with blades, bullets or shrapnel. The self is so within the skin in the paintings, and so carefully recreated, that damaging it would seem like sacrilege. As it happens, I can't bring to mind any of Freud's paintings that feature visibly damaged skin. There's skin of all ages, but no cuts, grazes or even bruises. Certainly no distressed and nibbled skin around the fingernails. No unhealed scabs on the knuckles. When the skin-as-self is as well attended to as this, the idea of hurting it seems appalling.

Contemplating skin-picking from the perspectives of both Benthien's categories initially suggests that the action should be considered distressing and damaging, plus counterproductive to reducing anxiety. Something inside me still rejects this hypothesis. Is there any way, I wonder, that picking at the skin could be understood as something other than straightforwardly destructive? To return to the idea of the skin as encasing the self, trying to strip back the body's outermost layers when feeling anxious is, it seems, baffling. But what if the anxiety that haunts me isn't related to feeling too much? What if it's the fear of not feeling enough? The worry that everything is gently or forcibly encouraging us to not feel; to build thicker layers around ourselves, to hide behind virtual or physical walls, to medicate away the feelings. Sometimes I'm scared of forgetting to feel things enough, to remember to pause and let in this moment of walking through the park, of me, of you, of the green that could almost never feel intense enough. As much as I want the world to give me less of the daily anxieties of digitised life, I also want it to give me more. More of something that I could bleed into and be saturated with in return. Art is an incubator of endless ideas exploring what would happen if we opened ourselves up to the environment or to each other. Art provides images that make real the question: what happens when boundaries dissolve as we refuse to see the edges as edges?

In November 2016, while I was reviewing a festival of performance art, I stumbled across *Union* by Hellen Burrough and Philip Bedwell. In the short piece, the two performers, who are also married, silently stitch connective threads through their skin as they stand naked in front of the audience. The work explores how seminal events in our lives often become inscribed on the skin in the form of scars or other marks. But by puncturing the skin, Burrough and Bedwell suggest that to truly connect to another human, as in a marriage or other relationship, we need the boundaries encasing us to become porous and, with that, to endure the threat of pain laced through such vulnerability. At the centre of the work is the idea of trust: if either performer were to step suddenly backward, they could cause the other considerable pain by ripping the needles out of the skin. Yet by deliberately designing a scenario that could end in agony, Burrough and Bedwell achieve a surprising expression of tenderness.

The ideas underpinning *Union* work just as well whichever understanding of skin one accepts. Either the potency of the piece lies in the idea of perforating the skin to reveal the hidden self, or it lies in breaking open the skin-as-self to better connect with another human. It's this idea of connections that intrigues me. Is it possible that picking at the skin is a manifestation of yearning? A habitual reminder of a desire, almost greed, to consume more of everything? Perhaps it's also a need to express thoughts, memories and ideas without filters, conventions of politeness or foreknowledge of what is or isn't appropriate to share. A rejection, really, of the boundaries that exist between us. Is it that I want you under my skin?

Sonant

Eley Williams

I am an editor of laughs.

~~Let me try that again; no point trying to make the role seem more interesting than the reality.~~ I am a sound editor. I always hope to be *sound* in the same way that an argument is *sound* – *sound* as in *good foundations* – but what I mean is that I edit sounds at my place of work. I am in charge of monitoring canned laughter before it is added to a TV programme's audio tracks. When I'm introduced to strangers and talk about my job I tend to find myself making small *snip snip* motions in the air by way of illustration. I regret doing this almost instantly but try not to let this show on my face until I am back home, playing back the rushes in my head and rescanning the reels of the day. There in the dark I remember the way that my hands imitated scissors or snapping clapperboards mid-conversation. You had smiled as I snipped the air. It was a warm smile, I remember. It was the warmest thing at a cold dinner party. I replay the scene, your warmth and my snipping, and my bedroom ceiling frowns back at me.

Thanks to my line of work I've heard all kinds of laughs and grown accustomed to their different shapes and flavours, their unique anatomies. The bucking laughs, the buckling laughs, the explosive and the emphatic and the frantic, the muffled: *HAH*, *ha ha*, *ahahahaha*, *ha-hah*, *ooo-a*, *BWHUH*, **ha**, *ha*, *ha*, (ha), 'ha', *whuhuh*, *zchuh*, [nasal seethe], *heh*, *hoh*!, *hh*, *ssSSSSSss-s-s*. Aaa. I suppose I've never heard a bona fide teehee in the wild but like a birdwatcher waiting in their hide I welcome its appearance some day. I find it hard to imagine a real teehee: sharp splutters are rarely attenuated into vowelled wheezes. 'Teehee,' I say very clearly to my bathroom mirror and watch my eyebrows and the corners of my mouth for signs of genuine mirth. It seems more like a sprightly kind of sigh. A wheedling *tsk*.

I only hear the laughs and have to imagine what the laugher would have looked like when producing such a noise. I take sly field-notes when I'm out of the office. Some people tip their heads back and laugh with hidden loops and stripes of colour in their throat, flattening their tongues and winching their lips in, shoulders juddering: *can can can*. This is a laugh that uses the diaphragm and I think is slightly frightening in its velocity, as if the joke has become lodged in the windpipe and one is struggling to unseat it. Laughter as expectorate, or the laugh as a tickling, swallowed moth or wishbone.

Someone in the studio's sound booth at work had taken the time to stick a faux-motivational poster to the carpeted wall above the sound deck. It is a simple A4 piece of paper with a Bible quotation printed on it in big black letters, impossible to ignore above my monitor.

'Ha, Ha'

– *Book of Job*, Chapter 39:Verse 25 (King James Version)

I wonder if the quality of this transliterated laugh changes depending on which edition of the Bible you use. I made a mental note to check if any editors decided against the dry exclamatory 'Ha, ha' and plumped for a 'Teehee'. Some wag had written 'JOB SATISFACTION' next to the quotation in red biro. I laughed the first time I clocked that, a skiffling type of sniffle or sniffling type of skiffle springing unbidden from my nose. Somebody else had added a smiley face in thick marker beneath the quotation. Their marker must have been an old one because the upsilon slid-horseshoe of the smiley's mouth tapered off into a scattered scratch of ink. You had to be looking very closely at the poster to catch this detail. I only noticed because I was stood on tiptoe and leaning right over the monitor and mixing desk, squinting as umpteen laughs played toothily, toothlessly, tunelessly through my headphones and through my head.

One night while I tried to stare-down my bedroom ceiling, wondering for the thousandth time why on earth I had thought it was necessary to mime my job title to someone at a party with that silly *snip snip* gesture, it struck me that the phrase is *canned* laughter rather than *tinned*. I wondered whether the difference was important. What else is *canned*? *Canned* can mean *binned*. Whoop-ass comes in cans, doesn't it, rather than by the binful or baleful or sachet or tin? *Tinny* laughter has other connotations after all. What do I know about the canning process? Turning in my bed, I imagined the meat and legs of teehee-moths being spat free from audience members' throats and strimmed away, hydrojetted through a microphone's grille so it can be pulped and squeezed through the wires in my headphones.

Another thought intruded: someone at a *snip snip* dinner party once cornered me into a three-hour conversation about organic farming, and I remember them saying too-close to my face the sentence: 'If the animals are distressed, the adrenaline in the muscles can be tasted in the meat.' I did not know what to say in response. Possibly I gave a nervous laugh, a small white butterfly released into a gale. The line about toxins and ruined flesh made something beneath my own skin stiffen. I imagined the canned meat of a mothy, mealy-mouthed laugh being scooped up, compacted, seasoned, labelled and made ready for consumption.

Across the landing, I heard an insect headbutting the bathroom light. It was a thoughtless percussion. The best laughs that I've ever had all caught me unawares, stealing up from my ribs and pinching my eyes into surprised tears. These laughs did not rely on calculation or hyper-attentiveness, nor any pre-prepared *snip snip* gestures. True laughs are unwitting creatures, a communication of delight that comes without forethought. You have to close your eyes as you make such a laugh as if it is a too-bright thing.

Every day, the leaden stilted false laugh above my work desk:

Ha, Ha.

The sheen of tin is so close to silver but cheaper and duller. Easier to produce. Tinny laughs are prized less than silvery laughs, I thought, as the meat of my arms began to relax.

'There's a line from Bergson about the social function of laughter,' said the man at the dinner party, pretending he was interested in my job by telling me he had a more interesting angle on it. He had the look of a man who recited Bergson by heart to people who stabbed the air between dinner guests with scissor-like hands. He also had the look of a man whose adrenaline would never ruin his meat. I envied him as I made my snip snip gesture, not knowing how to respond other than by releasing another small white butterfly of a laugh as he drew his face nearer.

It is just a dinner party, I tell myself. *This is not a frightening thing.*

Perform not being frightened at a dinner party for no reason. I continued and concentrated on widening my smile. The lights in the room all felt very bright and winked oddly off the cutlery and off the teeth and in the eyes of the man speaking to me.

There were all kinds of laughter around us in this heaving, genteel, tin-silvery room: some laughs were sludgy with drink but had the bite of desire. Some laughs curdled, others scattered like shot. *Just a dinner party.* Some laughs squatted on guests' chests like something from a Fuseli painting or clambered into ears like heavy-footed gargoyles. Others curved meteoric arcs of delicate frost across the table.

A *claque* is an organized body of professional applauders that are paid to appear in French theatres. For a split second, I imagined something similar was happening here: people had been planted to simulate real laughs and had made a bet that no two would be alike.

'Shall I tell it to you?' the man said.

'Ha, ha—'

Someone across the room chose that moment to give a laugh that was impossible to pin down: it sounded desperate while also plummy and full, and edged with an undeniable horror. Tantalus looking at the suspended fruit from the chill of the river and getting a grip of himself. All around us laughs bounced off teeth and wine glasses, hid in the folds of napkins and curtains, jockeyed on the pendulum of the mantelpiece clock. It made my head spin. Behind the man's ear, in that moment, I saw the room in total silence: without sound, with heads tilted upwards and snapping at the hinges, I saw laughs performed as if each dinner guest was taking greedy, rough bites of the air.

I watched the man opposite me smile as he quoted his philosopher, watched his mouth tightening a fraction with a pursing of pride. I did not catch a word over the laughing roar.

I remember that I nodded and released another laugh-butterfly. Its wings were ragged and the laugh slipped from between my teeth in a stumbling gawky flight, playing the clown as a defensive mechanism. It was a different species to my first laugh: nervous laughs are not the same as forced ones.

The man leaned further in. 'There's more!' he said.

The butterflies snipped the air between us with their wings.

'"The billows clash and collide with each other," he continued, '"as they strive to find their level. A fringe of snow-white foam, feathery and frolicsome, follows their changing outlines.'"

The man looked at me, expecting congratulation.

Beyond his shoulder, I saw you notice that I was trapped. You had overheard the conversation and caught my line of sight – to save me, and make me laugh, I saw you roll your eyes.

Breath left my body unbutterflied, grateful, unchecked.

At work the next day, leaning over my monitor, I took a pencil from behind my ear and squared my shoulders. A new laughter track was in my headphones where it pounded like waves, inking along the folds of my brain. I narrowed my eyes and drew the exclamation marks onto the poster with strong, sure lines.

Ha! Ha!

Black Girl Healing: Making it Better

Marianne Tatepo

It is a thing of hearts in throats, of throats in knots, of knots in stomachs. A thing of restless brains, sleepless nights, ends that feel nigh. A thing of breathlessness, recurring appointments, endless symptoms. That is how I can best describe my second in command. We are pretty tight, now – me and Anxiety; Anxiety and me.

Living together has been a learning curve, although I couldn't say things *get* better. Instead, through time, talking and mental discipline I found ways to make myself feel better. This comes with the baggage of my blackness, my womanhood, orientation, education, class and employment. Those elements feature heavily here but I speak of our universal anxious leanings. I want to tell you about what happened, what I did and what I learned, in the hope it makes you feel less powerless, or understood, or that it makes you understand. This volume has a resource of organisations that can assist, places to go and things to do to heal at the end.

A Standing Appointment

We meet in late winter, when I think I have just about got my shit together. I pretend we are not acquainted. By spring I must Talk To Someone – my second in command insists that, for the first time ever, I cannot cope with all my responsibilities. I email the relevant people as soon as I realise life is moving too fast and I am referred to someone who they say can help. No overtime on Tuesdays; I clock out at 5.30pm on the dot for a 6.30pm session, a constant in an otherwise uncertain future. 'I have a standing appointment...' I hint at those who matter on paper. Those who do in my heart are made aware. Perhaps my therapist – I have never called her that before – could really *get* me this time. It is luck, me getting her. Luck and misfortune colliding: there have been several crises that led to me sharing my innermost concerns with strangers for 50 minutes. One recurring slot had been on Saturday morning. Another from 8 to 9pm on Friday night. I'd join post-work drinks for 'just one' and those who knew me to be a banterous colleague observed me deep in thought, unsettled by my lack of liver destruction. Or I'd meet friends, still wrapped up in my own cumulus.

In those days, kinship, even if just in impression, truly mattered. My grandmother had just died. Then, on return from the burial in Cameroon, which I couldn't afford to attend, my mother fell ill and was admitted to hospital. With this accumulation of hectic office days, academic duties and unexpressed grief, I once more found myself in an armchair, staring at the tentative tissue box, my mind a continent away. But for the first time – after a lifetime of no authority figures in my life other than my family being thus – that stranger was a black woman.

***

In Plato's eponymous allegory, prisoners who live shackled in the darkness of the cave are unable to see others and themselves properly; they only see shadows. Their vision of humanity is not only partial, it is erroneous. When a prisoner escapes the cave, they are stunned by the depth of the objects and shapes they perceive in this new reality. While the takeaway is typically that philosophers, as technocrats, are berated for their ability to know more than the general populace, this also indicates the lesser existence of those unable to see themselves and others in a complex manner. Here, a parallel can be drawn with representation. In Western societies, many of which have been rendered multiracial through centuries of expeditions (i.e. rape, pillage and assimilation), the topic is at once underrated and treasured. Representation is a birthright and a threat for those in a position to take it for granted. See the backlash following the depiction of a black father as the head of a Roman family in a historical BBC cartoon, even as this has been corroborated by classicist Mary Beard and other historians as consistent with the Roman Empire's capacious aspirations stretching into the African continent. This is the typical response of those who seemingly view history, the media and humanity as no more than a broadsheet, in which both people and historical accounts come in one size only, limited run.

Due to its ability to counter such views, Issa Rae's HBO show *Insecure* is important to many young black women. Issa, the lead, is charismatic, funny and, crucially, three-dimensional in her fallibility. Likewise, her straight-talking best friend, high-flying lawyer and romantic perfectionist Molly, is afforded complexity, in particular with regards to mental health. In season two (spoiler) these traits take her into the pristine, book-laden office of a demure grey-haired middle-aged therapist with a buzz cut. A black woman. It is not explicit how Molly stumbles upon her – this ellipsis demonstrates how much more visible black communities are in the US. But it also indicates that Molly's socio-economic status allowed such access. Their racial and gender match does not prevent a brief fallout a few sessions into their relationship, but on the whole Molly finds relief in the shorthand of shared systemic oppression.

In *Citizen*, Jamaican writer Claudia Rankine writes, unforgettably: 'The new therapist specialises in trauma counselling. You have only ever spoken on the phone ... When the door finally opens, the woman standing there yells, at the top of her lungs, "Get away from my house! What are you doing in my yard?"' In 2016, the *Guardian* published a feature entitled 'Your therapist is white. You're not. Is this a problem?' In the investigation, a black man mentions a desire for a 'black male therapist from an upper-class background from New York' – an identity that mirrors his. This need is later met and he mentions a past experience with a white female therapist where he felt he was handled like a threat: 'She shut me down when I expressed anger.' Conversely, his experience with his black male therapist is so positive it convinces him to pursue the profession.

Likewise, I had come across deadpan white women counsellors and men, like those described by a woman from the feature who identifies as Latina, looking 'like that suburban dad that you see on TV'. A Jon Ronson, a Louis Theroux. My three previous counsellors had their own respective professional and personal merit, still none appeared to relate to the issues I faced. I started considering gender and race as joint prejudices. With one woman, the differences at hand felt too pronounced for me to be handled efficiently – they were lost in translation. I expressed this awkwardly to a friend and was pegged as, loosely, self-important. I nearly believed them. Then along came Sophie.

Love & Death

Sophie came into my life after Mr ThirstTrap, and right after Grandma's passing. Mr ThirstTrap hadn't been loved and he hadn't loved right back. Even so, he had sent my heart looping inside my chest. The first panic attack I remember is one of limerence, these feelings so interwoven in my mind. We were stood in my kitchen sharing Spanish wine and mischiefs after not having met in six weeks. Emails ranging a panoply of emotions had been exchanged – lust had come out on top, as had he. The conversation came back to our togetherness, or rather, lack thereof. I being coyly pro, he playfully contra, the mutual pull centrifugal whichever way. We sat by my windowsill and when it became evident that we were going nowhere, not then and perhaps never, I found myself trembling, unable to breathe, my stomach in knots, bile rising up my throat. This was the first time that I realised my body could expose me unawares. He wrapped himself around me and reassured me it was ok and it was his fault everything was this complicated, while I wondered what we were to do about 'us', knowing this word to be too populous for these unrequited feelings.

I saw the worst douchebags of my generation destroy girls like me by using white fragility as a way to establish romantic desirability. Sensitivity, although a key trait of mine, was foreign to me after two decades spent with boys referring to me as threatening, saying things like 'I would never mess with her because she could beat me up.' They would offer to walk my white girl friends home, while I was sent off alone because 'I am strong'; misogynoir stereotypes used to mask physical neglect.

One day, on the maple counter of Mr ThirstTrap's sitting room I found a book that read 'Overcoming Anxiety'. It felt like a confession from him but something irrelevant to me. I forgot then the time when I shook and fell into him as though he were a lake and I a willow. It took another two years until I Talked To Someone.

***

It has always felt to me like my purpose is to make others well. When the call that broke my life in two – before death had touched me and after – came I had the flu and had just been sent home. My sister called but wouldn't talk. She insisted, 'Just call me when you get home.' At home I called her. 'So… grandma has died. I am sorry,' she said. My reply was stilted. 'Oh. Right. Ok…So Mum isn't well… Ok.' My eyes welled up. 'Ok. I – I'll call her.' I'm not sure how long I slept for or what happened next.

In the month following my grandmother's passing I could do little more than be with my phone on loudspeaker and join my mother's crying. But calling Europe was pricey. After a couple weeks of silence when my parents didn't answer their home phone or mobiles, I was finally told that they had travelled to Cameroon – something I had not known them to be able to afford, what with the €1500 airfare from Brussels. After accepting the silence of grief, I focused on academia and work. I did not hear from them for two more weeks. Then one day, stepping out of the shower, I received a Whatsapp message: 'Mum is in hospital. She fell sick during the funeral.' I collapsed onto my bed naked, breathless at what felt like an inevitability: she was next. I couldn't face that. The next week was unbearable. A weight sat on my chest and my breath was faint but I said nothing, for fear of being seen to bring my problems into work. But at our weekly team meeting my eyes glistened when my boss asked 'Anyone got any news to share?'. I was given compassionate leave and took a seven-hour bus home. My mother had been released the night before, after a week as an in-patient. She was frail and, for once, awfully quiet. I lay next to her like day one, our hearts and breathing in sync.

I have spent most of my life learning not to obsess over my parents' deaths and my own as an imminent threat. There is precedent. One of my parents was diagnosed with a chronic illness at my birth and the other became ill with cancer when I was a teen. This meant regular hospital visits and clinical trials that sucked the energy out of them. I learned to feel comfortable in a hospital or sickbed, although I treat hospitals like corridors not rooms. I prayed to the relevant parties and when they refused to hear me I relegated them to faraway crevices in my mind – regaled them with a silent treatment yet to be lifted.

Marianne Tatepo

(Psycho)Therapy for Beginners

Perhaps not having God just threw me into the hands of another institution that collects my money. But there was something different about Sophie. Psychotherapy puts talking at the centre of the practice. A counselor had previously initiated Psychodynamic Therapy, where the bones of your past trauma are dug up and smeared all over your face. However, Sophie practiced Cognitive Behavioural Therapy, an NHS favourite due to its fixed-term nature. The NHS offers six-week sessions where you – alone or as a group – learn about mechanisms that can shield you from emotional harm. By recognising what your central belief system is and your behaviour patterns or logic, your therapist should offer solutions as to how to react to the situations that leave you feeling negatively. At the time, I was writing a thesis while working full-time and had to deal with unaddressed emotional abuse both present and past. Sophie and I spoke about different experiences, romantically, platonically, with family, friends, and at work, to identify my perceived position in the world and challenge harmful beliefs.

A key takeaway is that while anxiety primarily manifests as a physical and emotional disturbance, it can also mean your brain is wired differently. Those with Generalised Anxiety Disorder experience 'overgeneralisation'. Their brain interprets threatening and non-threatening situations similarly as a 'better safe than sorry' strategy. While this can create a lot of anxiety, it is an evolutionary advantage – those people are probably less likely to die from one of those 'do you trust me' tenth-storey Facebook challenges where people take videos of loved ones hanging from skyscrapers. This response comes from the brain's fear centre, the amygdala. This is the same organ that regulates feelings of infatuation, creating the same response as anxiety, according to the book *On Romantic Love: Simple Truths about a Complex Emotion*.

I cannot rewire myself fully, but with Sophie (and here I think of the skits on SZA's album *Ctrl*) I learned to forgo my sense of control where it was an illusion, explored the question 'What's the worst that could happen?' and let my worries run their course, convincing myself I would find solutions as and when issues did materialise – mostly, they didn't. My six months with Sophie, which I paid for at a negotiated £40 a session, worked well enough for me to be unable to summon the distress now. They gave me lifelong tools to deal with daily challenges. At the time I was able to spend £160 a month on my mental health – although we switched to fortnightly sessions as my wallet dried up. Many do not have that luxury. This was the first instance of my paying at the point of access. Previously I had benefitted from institutions offering complimentary six-week runs. But my ultimately positive experience with Sophie cannot speak for the system, which by and large needs adjustments.

The (Colourblind) Problem with Therapy

In her column 'How Well-Meaning Therapists Commit Racism', psychologist Monnica Williams PhD writes that the 'largest predictors of dissatisfaction in African American clients [is racial microaggressions]'. Shose Kessi, a South African psychologist and academic writes about decolonising psychology as a catalyst for social change. Kessi galvanises practitioners to 'no longer take refuge in knowledge projects or academic work'. In other words, to not only read from the canon of recognised Western thinkers on the subjects of psychology and psychoanalysis but also from alternative cultural artefacts from non-white cultures. Otherwise 'aren't we simply assisting people to adapt to and survive in oppressing living conditions?' To illustrate instances where psychology has looked further afield to meet the needs of patients, he quotes the existence of feminist, postcolonial and liberation psychology – all of which investigate relations of power between groups in society and treat people as diverse, fluid and part of intersecting systems of oppression.

This rings just as true in the UK. According to mentalhealth.org, 'African-Caribbean people living in the UK have lower rates of common mental disorders than other ethnic groups but are more likely to be diagnosed with severe mental illness ... [and] are also more likely to enter the mental health services via the courts or the police, rather than from primary care, which is the main route to treatment for most people.' In the latest report from mental health charity MIND ('We Still Need to Talk: A Report on Access to Talking Therapies', November 2013), it is acknowledged that 'people from BME communities have long been underserved in primary mental health services and are much less likely to be referred to psychological therapies'. Key concerns include how therapy interacts with religion or spirituality, as well as language barriers.

It becomes obvious that multicultural and inclusive education is necessary for practitioners – there is an urgent need for cultural relativism, where it does not interfere with core human rights. Indeed, even for those of us with primarily Westernised values, we cannot erase our various cultures. In a *Broadly* article, journalist Yomi Adegoke explores the young black women who have reverted to ancestral African religions for healing and as a further way to decolonise black spiritual institutions. For those reasons, I find it essential to research different psychotherapy methods, in particular associations that are dedicated to specific groups of people of colour – do consult the resource at the end of this book.

Feeling Good

Therapy isn't for everyone and it isn't forever, therefore DIY is an essential tool. Self-care has been reappropriated away from the peers of pioneer Audre Lorde, straight into the hands of the elites of the Anglophone West. It is increasingly a viral spectacle, co-opted by the insouciants of the middle and upper-middle classes. I am skipping introductions as Lorde speaks for herself, but her stance on black womanhood bears repeating: 'Caring for myself is not self-indulgence, it is self-preservation, and that is an act of political warfare.'

Just as with activism, self-care requires a degree of conspicuousness. We need broader representation of black women in positions of non-fetishised power, less of the same 'angry black woman' trope. From *Insecure's* Issa being indecisive, to *Scandal's* Olivia Pope crying into a wine glass the size of her head over the beau she last lost, the visibility of simple human weakness is important to the full depiction of black women's humanity and individuality. Because when you come from the rib of Adam, you sometimes forget to live for the sake of Eve.

At Edinburgh Book Festival, author and feminist Chimamanda Ngozi Adichie told First Minister Nicola Sturgeon growing older is a case of 'looking in the bag of fucks to give and finding it's empty'. It took two decades of understanding myself merely as a portion – daughter of, (black) friend of, or, more rarely, girlfriend of – to realise that I am a full person. The worry associated purely with the perception of others was exhausting. Anxiety's fucked-up tests taught me this much: I am my own person first and foremost, and my body and my joy belong to me. It taught me to not feel guilt when ensuring whatever I do or don't for the benefit of others wouldn't sabotage me. Self-care needs to be visible – not as a flaunt but as an inspiring reminder of the worth of the many the health and beauty industries erase and undermine.

Pep Talk

Body & Mind

Much like editing, as one of many ways to look after myself, exercise feels great once I have done it. When I do, my weapons of choice are swimming and the cross trainer, while the rowing machine is good when I can handle blisters. Speaking of blisters, guitar always helps to soothe me and though I sing badly, I can play ok – but it doesn't matter, what does is learning a thing for its sake. Dreadlocks swim caps have changed my relationship with the swimming pool – a scalp saver. But the body is often a trap, too. Nowadays, rather than feeling bad on days I don't exercise, I try to sit for ten minutes before bed and breathe in and out, as calmly as possible, while stretching lightly and remember the things that made me smile that day. *Ad nauseam*.

When my body wants to rest, I call upon my brain alone. Reading essays somehow always captivates me and slows my heart rate down, while the theatre excites me. The Soho Theatre is an excellent venue, with wheelchair access. It has unwittingly become one of my havens. It is at the forefront in bringing powerful performances that cover anything from sexual assault to pop icons, via sexuality, anxiety and depression. Chris Gethard's irreverence in 'Career Suicide', Bryony Kimmings's musicality in 'Fake it Till You Make It', and Le Gateau Chocolat's sequinned baritone contrast left their mark on anxious me. My only resolution this year was to see one comedy (show) a month. But when I haven't planned or cannot afford to see a live show, I have decided Netflix will do. Entertainment is at the core of well-being.

Overthinking can be harmful. But what has helped me is having at least one half hour a day to sit with my thoughts: the good, the bad and the confusing. I ask myself how I feel, what I want, and why. I write it down either way, and reflect. Airplane mode does wonders; my phone has a curfew. I'm learning to be patient with myself because this is the only brain and body I will have. This is how our neurological system works. Anxiety is just a different way in which we see the world. Anxiety makes me more attuned to the movement around me. The whispers and brewing news, I notice the little cues and connect the clues, learning when to dismiss or engage with their negativity. Think about how these heightened sensations may help 'Anxies' (now it's a thing) to perceive more than others and how we can use this to our advantage. It's an evolutionary advantage, damn it! But for all the mechanisms...

'Don't live your life in fear.'

Recently, during a call where I disclosed my struggles to my mother, she simply said this. Mental health can be taboo among people of colour. Immigrant's guilt: as a rule, I'd sooner struggle alone and resolve my problems than 'burden' the family that move thousands of miles north for me to prosper, which can lead to an isolated accumulation of distress and sadness. These words came to me like the missing piece of a puzzle I had been sat on. My fear of failure and judgement had hurt me most – acceptance and empathy relieved me of months of, ultimately, fretting. Poet Anaïs Nin wrote 'Anxiety is love's biggest killer' in her diary – I reject that idea. It's sound bites like my mother's that make one's strength. Talking to loved ones matters just as much and can even strengthen relationships. From our anxious minds, we worry there is a chance they will make us feel worse. But what if they don't? Anxiety is the maybe that distracts you from that which is; trying to be well is half the battle won.

Resources

[editor's note: Marianne includes below some resources she used and found helpful. We have more resources at the end of the book on page 147]

Sometimes when there is too much going on it can feel overwhelming to research things. To make things a little easier, I have compiled a list of articles of resources for you. These are videos, and books consulted while writing this volume.

On anxiety and neurology

The 15 Best TED Talks On Anxiety, Stress, and Fear
http://athingnamed.com/best-ted-talks-on-anxiety-stress-and-fear/

'CBT Changes the Brain' King's College London, January 2017, excerpted from Mason, L et al (2017) 'Brain connectivity changes occurring following cognitive behavioural therapy for psychosis predict long-term recovery Translational Psychiatry'
https://www.kcl.ac.uk/ioppn/news/records/2017/January/Study-reveals-for-first-time-that-talking-therapy-changes-the-brain's-wiring.aspx

'Your words may predict your future mental health', Mariano Sigman, TED 2016:https://www.ted.com/talks/mariano_sigman_your_words_may_predict_your_future_mental_health

'Decolonising psychology creates possibilities for social change', Shose Kessi, The Conversation, September 2016 http://theconversation.com/decolonising-psychology-creates-possibilities-for-social-change-65902

'How anxiety scrambles your brain and makes it hard to learn', Juliet Rix, *Guardian*, November 2015
https://www.theguardian.com/education/2015/nov/21/how-anxiety-scrambles-your-brain-and-makes-it-hard-to-learn

On therapy and ethnicity

Decolonizing "Multicultural" Counseling through Social Justice, editors: Rachael D. Goodman, Paul C. Gorski, (Springer, 2015)
http://www.springer.com/gp/book/9781493912827

'Decolonizing Academia: Intersectionality, Participation, and Accountability in Family Therapy and Counseling', Teresa McDowell and Pilar Hernández, Family Therapy and Counseling', *Journal of Feminist Family Therapy*, 22: 2, 93 - 111, May 2010
http://www.lclark.edu/live/files/5661

'How Therapists Drive Away Minority Clients' Monnica T Williams PhD, *Psychology Today*, June 2013
https://www.psychologytoday.com/blog/culturally-speaking/201306/how-therapists-drive-away-minority-clients

'Talking About Race in Trauma', by Garrett B. Work, M.A., Riley Cropper, M.A., & Constance J. Dalenberg, Ph.D., The Society for the Advancement of Psychotherapy
http://societyforpsychotherapy.org/talking-about-race-in-trauma-psychotherapy/

'Your therapist is white. You're not. Is this a problem?', Rose Hackman, *Guardian*, May 2016
https://www.theguardian.com/science/2016/may/28/finding-good-therapist-gender-race-cultural-competency

'What happens in the brain when we experience a panic attack?', Paul Li and Jeannine Stamatakis, *Scientific American*, July 2011 https://www.scientificamerican.com/article/what-happens-in-the-brain-when-we-experience/

'I Have Chronic Anxiety, And This Is How My Brain Works', Andrea Wesley, XO JANE, September 2016 http://www.xojane.com/healthy/i-have-chronic-anxiety-brain

'The Brains of Anxious People May Perceive the World Differently', Kate Horowitz, *Mental Floss*, March 2016 http://mentalfloss.com/article/76694/brains-anxious-people-may-perceive-world-differently

'Researchers discover how the brain turns chronic stress into pathological anxiety', Scripps Research Institute, Science Daily, February 2017
https://www.sciencedaily.com/releases/2017/02/170213131201.htm

'Racial Microaggressions and the Therapeutic Encounter', Kristine Miranda, UPenn Repository, May 2013 http://repository.upenn.edu/cgi/viewcontent.cgi?article=1053&context=edissertations_sp2

On self-care

'Generation treat yo' self: the problem with 'self-care'', Arwa Mahdawi, *Guardian*, January 2017 https://*www*.theguardian.com/lifeandstyle/2017/jan/12/self-care-problems-solange-knowles

'Self-care ain't what it used to be and other news', Dan Piepenbring, *The Paris Review*, December 2016 https://www.theparisreview.org/blog/2016/12/12/self-care-aint-what-it-used-to-be-and-other-news/

'Self-care as Warfare', Sara Ahmed, FeministKilljoy blog, August 2014
https://feministkilljoys.com/2014/08/25/selfcare-as-warfare/

'The Politics of self-care', Jordan Kisner, *The New Yorker*, March 2017
http://www.newyorker.com/culture/culture-desk/the-politics-of-selfcare

'11 self-help books written by black people that will get you through anything', Ebony F, Blavity, January 2017
https://blavity.com/self-help-books-written-by-black-people-that-will-get-you-through-anything/?utm_content=bufferaf4bf&utm_medium=social&utm_source=facebook.com&utm_campaign=buffer

On love

'Love on the brain', Roger Dobson, *The Independent*, October 2010 http://www.independent.co.uk/news/science/love-on-the-brain-2096672.html

'Love is like cocaine: The remarkable, terrifying neuroscience of romance', Berit Brogaard, *Salon*, February 2015
http://www.salon.com/2015/02/14/love_is_like_cocaine_the_remarkable_terrifying_neuroscience_of_romance/

Me I.R.L.

Siobhan Britton

Resources

Anxiety UK

Anxiety UK is a user-led organisation, run by people with experience of living with anxiety, stress or anxiety-based depression, supported by a high-profile medical advisory panel. Their website includes resources on anxiety and comorbid issues, and has a therapist directory.
www.anxietyuk.org.uk

The Black, African and Asian Therapy Network (BAATN)

BAATN is the UK's largest independent network of therapists who specialise in working with Black, African, Asian and Caribbean people. Their website lists a therapist directory and resources.
www.baatn.org.uk

Centre for Mental Health

Centre for Mental Health's aim is to change the lives of people with mental health problems by using research to bring about better services and fairer policies.
www.centreformentalhealth.org.uk

Childline UK

A confidential helpline specifically for children and young people. The website has a number of resources and message boards, specifically for young people. They also have support phone lines and resources for parents.
Helpline - call 0800 111 or you can use their website to instant chat or send an email to an advisor.
www.childline.org.uk/get-support/

Counselling Directory

The Counselling Directory was launched in 2005, and lists over 10,000 qualified counsellors and psychotherapists. The website also includes a number of resources on mental health and therapies, and in 2017 launched a regular magazine called *Happiful*.
http://www.counselling-directory.org.uk/

It's Good To Talk

Ran by the British Association for Counselling & Psychotherapy (BACP), It's Good to Talk provides a comprehensive list of therapists and information on types of therapy available.
http://www.itsgoodtotalk.org.uk

Mental Health Foundation

The UK's charity for everyone's mental health, promoting good mental health for all.
www.mentalhealth.org.uk

Mind

Mind provides advice and support to empower anyone experiencing a mental health problem. They campaign to improve services, raise awareness and promote understanding. Mind has over 140 local groups across England and Wales.
www.mind.org.uk
Mind Helpline
Call: 0300 123 3393
Text: 86463

Rethink

Rethink Mental Illness provides advice and information to those affected by mental health problems. Rethink campaigns nationally for policy change and runs over 200 mental health services and 150 support groups across England.
www.rethink.org
Rethink Advice and Information Service
Call: 0300 5000 927 Open 10am to 2pm, Monday to Friday or e-mail advice@rethink.org

Samaritans

Samaritans offer a safe place to talk anytime you like, in your own way, about whatever's getting to you. They are available 24 hours a day.
www.samaritans.org
Samaritans Helpline
Call: 116 123
Email: jo@samaritans.org

SANE

SANE works to improve quality of life for anyone affected by mental health problems, including family, friends and carers.
www.sane.org.uk/
SANE Helpline
Call: 0300 304 7000
You can email them through their website.
Open 6pm - 11pm every day or you can email sanemail@sane.org.uk

Switchboard LGBT+ Helpline

A confidential helpline providing emotional support to LGBT+ people, ran by LGBT+ people. They are trans and nonbinary friendly.
www.switchboard.lgbt
Helpline - Call: 0300 330 0633 10am-10pm every day Email: chris@switchboard.lgbt
They also have an instant chat service through their website.

Time to Change

A growing social movement campaign changing how we all think and feel about mental health. They are run by Mind and Rethink Mental Illness.
www.time-to-change.org.uk

Young Minds

UK based charity committed to improving the wellbeing and mental health of children and young people.
www.youngminds.org.uk

My Anxious Mind: A Teen's Guide to Managing Anxiety and Panic by Michael A. Tompkins, Katherine A. Martinez & Michael Sloan, 9781433804502

Overcoming Anxiety: A Self-help Guide Using Cognitive Behavioral Techniques by Helen Kennerly, 9781849018784

Anxiety: Panicking about Panic: A powerful, self-help guide for those suffering from an Anxiety or Panic Disorder by Joshua Fletcher, 9781500117924

Our Authors & Artists

Shanicka Anderson is a Jamaican-American writer from New York. Often and without prompting, she enjoys talking pop culture, Harry Styles, her year abroad in London, and the complexities of the Caribbean diaspora.

Erin Aniker is a freelance illustrator based in London whose work is really influenced by the mixed female community she grew up with and her dual Turkish and English heritage. Most of her illustrations are completed digitally and have a big focus on celebrating women of diversity in colourful, minimalist environments. Erin enjoys creating illustrations for use across editorial, print and online platforms. You can view examples of her work on her website: www.erinaniker.com

Grace Au (them/they) is a part time jewellery-maker, part time writer, part time jack-of-all-trades. They have a degree in Design from Goldsmiths, University of London and are currently studying Architecture at Newcastle University. They spend their days thinking about memes, mental health, horror fiction, politics and using design to make life more accessible to everyone. You can buy their jewellry here: www.qruce.bigcartel.com

Ka Bradley is a writer and editor based in London. Her writing has appeared in *Granta*, *Under the Influence*, *Somesuch Stories*, *The Offing* and *Catapult*, among others. She reviews dance and theatre for *Exeunt*, londondance.com and *The Stage*, and is an editor at Granta Books and Portobello Books.

Siobhan Britton is an artist and librarian living in Brighton. She makes zines, comics and lino prints under the imprint Slug Ink Press. You can see more of her work on her blog www.librariankilljoy.wordpress.com and buy her work here
www.etsy.com/uk/shop/sluginkpress

Lori England is a writer and poet from Glasgow, Scotland. Her work has been published in *404 Ink*, by *Crab Fat Magazine* and was shortlisted for the 2015 Bold Types creative writing competition. She has recently completed her BA (Hons) in English Literature and Creative Writing at the Open University and juggles writing with bringing up her own tiny girl gang. You can find out more about her work on her website: www.loriengland.wordpress.com

Deborah Frempong is a writer and singer who lives in Boston by way of Accra, Ghana. She studied Politics at Pomona College and Religion at Harvard University. Her work has appeared in *Signatures Magazine*, *Cléo Journal*, the *Killens Review of Arts and Letters* and other publications. You can hear her music here: www.soundcloud.com/naakua1

Nicole Froio is a writer and Women's Studies PhD candidate at the University of York. She's Brazilian-Colombian and writes about pop culture, mental health, politics, feminism and books. She loves reading, writing and discovering new things.

Claire Gamble is queer, disabled and currently studying Fine Art in Nottingham. They run a blog at Retrogreat.com and are inspired by the Iron Age, because if you're going to go Retro, you may as well do it properly... You can find them on Twitter: @retrogreat

P.E. Garcia is a contributor to *HTMLGiant* and an Editor-at-Large for *The Rumpus*. They want to understand astrology.

Eli Goldstone is the author of *Strange Heart Beating* (Granta 2017). She lives in Margate and is a graduate of the City University Creative Writing MA.

Sarvat Hasin was born in London and grew up in Karachi. She studied Politics at Royal Holloway and Creative Writing at the University of Oxford. She is fiction editor at *The Stockholm Review* and works at Hachette Children's Group. Her debut novel, *This Wide Night*, has been published by Penguin India. It was recently longlisted for the DSC Prize for South Asian Fiction.

Amberin Huq is an author/illustrator born in Tooting, London to Bangladeshi parents. She studied illustration at Falmouth University in Cornwall and has been illustrating ever since. Amberin has created shows for Half Moon theatre as well as artwork for Polka Theatre, Little Angel Theatre and Theatre Royal Stratford and had her first children's book, *A Bump in the Night*, published in 2016 by Five Mile Press Australia. Although Amberin started in the children's market, she is now exploring the troubles of online dating in the modern age through the medium of short comics.

Dr. Rachel Kowert is a research psychologist from Austin, Texas, with a PhD in psychology from the University of York (UK) and an MA in counseling psychology from Santa Clara University. Dr. Kowert has dedicated her career to studying video games and the gamers who love them. She has been featured by *The Wall Street Journal, Polygon, Kotaku, New York Magazine's Science of Us* and Texas Public Radio among others. As a researcher, psychologist, gamer and parent, she strives to educate other parents about the potential dangers and unique contributions that video games can bring to our everyday lives. For more information, visit www.rkowert.com.

Sophie Mackintosh was born in South Wales, and is currently based in London. Her fiction and poetry has been published or is forthcoming in *Granta Magazine*, *The White Review* and *TANK Magazine*, amongst others. Her short story 'Grace' is the winner of the 2016 White Review Short Story Prize, and her story 'The Running Ones' won the Virago/Stylist Short Story competition in 2016. Sophie's debut novel *The Water Cure* is forthcoming in the UK & Canada from Hamish Hamilton, and in the US from Doubleday.

Narayani Menon is half Indian, a quarter English and a quarter Irish. Most of her previous writing has been for the stage; she is working on her first novel.

Alice Slater is a writer from London. She chairs the Waterstones Gower Street Short Story Salon and reviews short story collections for *Mslexia*. Her work has been shortlisted for the Bridport Prize. She tweets at @smokintofu.

Marianne Tatepo is child 9/9 of a Littoral and West Cameroonian family. Born and bred in Brussels, she is based in London and works in book publishing. Read Marianne's writing for the *Guardian*, the *Bookseller*, *Spread the Word*, *Brooklyn* magazine, and others here: www.mariannetatepo.com. Read her thoughts on books here: www.myliteraryplayground.com

Sharlene Teo is the winner of the inaugural Deborah Rogers Writer's Award for her debut novel *Ponti*, forthcoming from Picador and Simon & Schuster in 2018. She received the Booker Prize Foundation Scholarship and David T.K Wong Creative Writing award at the University of East Anglia, was recently shortlisted for the 2017 Berlin Writing Prize and holds fellowships from the Elizabeth Kostova Foundation and the University of Iowa International Writing Program.

Harriet Thompson is a writer and researcher interested in 19th and 21st century literary culture and women's life-writing. She is on the steering committee for literary magazine *Salomé* and is currently developing a podcast aimed at emerging writers.

Rosemary Waugh is a freelance writer and theatre critic. She is a co-owner and reviews editor for the independent online theatre magazine *Exeunt*. Alongside this, Rosemary regularly reviews theatre and dance for *The Stage* in the South West and Wales. She was recently invited to be a panellist for The Sick of the Fringe Festival at the Wellcome Collection, and a Critic in Residence at the Alchymy Festival of new playwriting. She likes to talk about gender, feminism and all the things that could go wrong with your body.

Eley Williams is a writer and lecturer based in London. Her collection of short stories *Attrib. And Other Stories* (Influx Press) was chosen by Ali Smith as one of the best debut works of fiction published in 2017. She has a collection of poetry *Frit* with Sad Press, and is currently co-editor of fiction at *3:AM magazine*.

Hannah Williams studied Literature in Sheffield and Stockholm, and now lives and writes in SE London. Her work has appeared in *The Skinny* among others. Her twitter handle is @handronicus.

Acknowledgements

This book would not have been possible without the support from our friends and family, the enthusiasm and hard work of our contributors and the generous pledges via Kickstarter. We would like to give special thanks to the following people:

Michael James Adams
Maria Aghdiran Marsh
Kate Ahl
Laura Alden
Andy Aldridge
Pam Andrews
Michael Amherst
David Arrowsmith
Melanie Ashford
Sophie Atkinson
Ant Attwood
Caden Bågenholm
David Bailey
Sarah Balmont
James Barlow
Emily Bater
Rob Benyer
Jennifer Bernstein
Carolyn Black
Amy Louise Blaney
Alice Bogen
Daniel Bogen
Morissa Bogen
Rachel Bogen Otero
Stephanie Boland
Lucy Bolton
Sally Bonneywell
Darren Bourget
Jessica Bowyer
Isabel Branco
Ruth Bridget Brennan
Matt Bridgeman-Rivett
Siobhan Britton
Catherine Brown
Nell Brown
Paul Burns
Nicole Burstein
Conor Byworth
& Lena Drotleff
Sophie Campbell
Elsa Carron
Sarah Carter
Henry Caushi
Malcolm Chisholm
Ruzina Choudhury
LC Clarke
Yvonne Clarke-Salt
Tom Clayton

Emma Coleman
Phoebe Colley
Philip Connor
Thomas Corker
Benjamin & Tilla Crowne
Theodora Danek
Rose de Lara
Jim Dean
Will Dean
Stephen Deutz
Robert Dingle
tom dissonance
Jenna Dobson
Emma Dolan
Hisham El-Far
Lauren Elkin
Laura Elliot
Lucie Elliott
Julie Emmanuel
Denise England
Norman Erikson Pasaribu
Tanis Eve
Victoria Eyton
Jessica Farish
Madeleine Fenner
Alice Field
Matt Flavell
Hannah "Er00" Fordham
Naomi French
Aisling Gallagher
Sarah Garnham
Josie George
Jo Godfrey
Dian Maisie Otter Grace
Jennifer Grant
Rob Gregg
Dan Hadley
Daniel Hahn
Theresa M. Hahn
Yvonne Han
Paul Hancock
Aidan Hanratty
Daniel Hansen
Jenny Harris
Kate Harrison
Rosalind Hayes
David Hebblethwaite
Maz Hedgehog
Erin Himrod
Rowan Hisayo Buchanan
Claire Holloway
Tomasz Hoskins
Bex Hughes
Graham Huws
Agri Ismaïl
krishanthi jeyakumar
Beth John
Tanya MB Johnson

Keith & Aliy Jones
Laura Joyce
Amy Key
Apola Kipso
Kelvin Kong
Kat Krusch
Patrick Langley
Fion J. Lau
Gayle Lazda
Howard J. Levenson
Chris Love
Danni Lutts
Esmee Maltby
Kuukuwa Manful
Karl Mathiesen
Fahad Mayet
Kathryn Maude
Superior Alex McDonald
Christina McDermott-McGarrigle (McMc)
Pete McGee
Emer McHugh
Katherine McMahon
Anna McNay
Marie-Anne McQuay
Annie Medz
Narayani Menon
Josie Michelle
Kiran Millwood Hargrave
Penny Montague
Glyn Morgan
Stephen Morrison
Beth Morris
Helen Victoria Murray
Vijay Nair
Tristan Alice Nieto
Sharon Nolan
Jo Norcup
Catherine Oakley
Emily Oram
Emily B. Owen
Joelle Owusu-Sekyere
Susie P
Josh Pappenheim
Ajay Patel
Thomas Peacock
Jane and Martin Pennington
Laura Pietrobon
Emily Pisacreta
Non Pratt
Alex Primavesi
Mary Ann Prior
Aaron Rackley
Alexa Radcliffe-Hart
Laura Renshaw
Laura Riley
Chris and Cathy Roberts
Eloise Roberts

Charlie Rodgers
Victoria Rodrigues O'Donnell
Matthew J. Rogers
Nicola Ryan
Michael Safranek
Kurt Schleier
Hazel Nico Shaw
Claire Shepherd
Sarah Shin
Shelley Shocolinsky-Dwyer
Elaine Simpson
Henry Slater
Becky Sliwa
Rebecca Spaven
R P Steeves
Isabella Streffen
Alice Stringer
Zeba Talkhani
Gemma Tasker
Janet Titchener
Hannah Trevarthen
Clemens Uittenbosch
Abbie Vickress
Francesca Wade
Rebecca Walsh
Sàmi Wannell
Lucian Waugh
Katherine Webber
Emily Wheeler
Emilie Morwenna Whitaker
Mark Whitehead
Jessie Widdowson
Amy Wilkerson
Beth Marie Williams
Claire Williams
Pip Williams
Tim Williams
Catherine Williamson
Ben Winston
Alex Withington-Smith
Alice Woods
Andrew Woods
Harriet Wragg
Jill Y

@christapus
Dani (@dani_reviews)
KS
Kyree
Stephen
PhilithD
Stephen
Dead Ink Books